"**OUTSTANDING, PHENOMENAL.** Rich blend of psychological insight, personal warmth and delightful sense of humor."

Elaine Haglund, Ph.D.
Department of Educational Psychology
California State University, Long Beach

"**FUN,** spirited style of presentation. Great ideas and personal insights. **OUTSTANDING!**"

Shirley Orechwa
School of Business Administration
University of Southern California

"**BEST IN THE BUSINESS.** Produces wonderful results with salesforce! A great theory that works! Inspirational and moving! Strongly recommended to all my friends. It will significantly impact your life."

Marie Mosteller
Training Coordinator
J. C. Penney Corporation

"**BREATH OF FRESH AIR.** Truly impressive message. Easily readable and easily understood. Changes lives."

Bruce Newlin, Ed.D.
Superintendent
Norwalk-La Mirada Unified School District

"**INCREDIBLE INSIGHTS.** The missing piece in the puzzle of relationships. What a difference *The Color Code* has already made in my personal, social and professional life."

Lee Bangerter
Chairman
Care Enterprises

How do I introduce this man? At first my thoughts turn to his many degrees and professional credentials. He has experienced so many things and enriched the hearts of so many people, and yet I find those degrees and credentials somewhat limited in introducing the *real* Taylor Hartman to you.

When I think of his doctoral degree at the United States International University in San Diego, California, I am more inclined to remember his commitment to his family and community obligations despite his heavy career and education schedule.

Taylor is a lover. He loves people so easily that one would almost have to live with him to appreciate how sincere his love is.

Taylor has always been committed to increasing the quality of life—not only his—but all of those he encounters. And yet, with this passion for Truth, he remains very playful and loves to live in the present.

Taylor is as comfortable playing "horsie" and "duck-duck-goose" in our family room, as he was recently addressing the International Congress of Psychologists in Austria. Infact, his playful behavior has often provided a creative outlet for our family. He dates each of our four daughters once a month and continues to romance me with frequent surprises and adventure.

Despite Taylor's busy professional counseling and consulting business, he still maintains that the highest compliment he ever received was from his nine year old daughter. She told her school teacher that she didn't mind having personal problems, because Dad would always take time to give her private counseling. Taylor has enjoyed many professional and civic responsibilities, and yet he always lets us know that we are the most important people in his life.

The question I am most often asked about Taylor is "What is it *really* like to live with him?" Perhaps the easiest and most accurate answer is to simply say, "He's a man who practices what he preaches."

The Color Code is a special gift from a very special person. He cares. This book will help you understand
- the mysteries of yourself
- the miracle of your relationships and,
- the magic of living

Taylor Hartman will touch your heart...This book will change your life...

Jean Hartman

The Color Code

A New Way To See
Yourself, Your Relationships And Life

By
Dr. Taylor Hartman

Preface

It happens to all of us. In social, business and even family encounters, we meet some people and instantly establish a rapport—laughing at the same things, concerned about the same issues, discovering, perhaps, that we have had similar life experiences. Then we meet others and just making conversation is a struggle—we're on guard, uncomfortable, inexplicably hostile.

Why?

In *The Color Code,* Dr. Taylor Hartman groups various aspects of personality and behavior into four color categories: Red, Blue, White and Yellow. While few of us are completely one color or another—we are potential rainbows within, Hartman writes—these categories represent a useful general guide to personality types.

Taylor Hartman color-codes personality because color is already a widely used metaphor for emotion and behavior. We "see red" when we're angry. We "feel blue" when we're sad. We turn "green with envy," which often brings on a "black mood."

Using Dr. Hartman's color guide to personality, readers will be able to establish and maintain relationships with greater ease—because they will "see" the motives behind their own and other peoples' behavior. They will be able to accept others for what they are. And, most important, they will learn to incorporate within themselves the best of all of the colors of life.

Table of Contents

Introduction

Chapter 1: The Elements of Personality — 1

—Personality is innate.
—Personality is an interpretation of life.
—Personality is a code of behavior.
—Personality is a mystery.
—Personality is a rainbow.

Chapter 2: Personality Profile Test — 6

—A 45-item multiple-choice personality test.
—A guide to interpreting test results—and understanding personality—in terms of the four color types: Red, Blue, White and Yellow.

Chapter 3: Color-Coded Motives — 15

—An overview of the motives and aspirations of each of the four personality types.

Chapter 4: Reds: The Power Wielders — 23

—A comprehensive accounting of the characteristics, attitudes, strengths, limitations and behavior patterns of Red personalities.
—How to avoid conflict and develop a positive relationship with a Red.

Chapter 5: Blues: The Do-Gooders — 40

—A comprehensive accounting of the characteristics, attitudes, strengths, limitations and behavior patterns of Blue personalities.
—How to avoid conflict and develop a positive relationship with a Blue.

Chapter 6: Whites: The Peace Keepers — 55

—A comprehensive accounting of the characteristics, attitudes, strengths, limitations and behavior patterns of White personalities.
—How to avoid conflict and develop a positive relationship with a White.

Introduction

February 14, 1986.

Ambulances and fire engines with flashing red lights and blaring sirens raced to the scene of our head-on collision. It was raining heavily that night. My wife and I had been out to dinner for Valentine's Day. She had recommended that we wear seat belts for the drive home. Twenty-five minutes later, I lay unconscious in my wife's lap while the fire fighters cut through the car door in an effort to free us and transport us to the hospital.

Not more than three months earlier we had moved to our dream home in the country in Southern California. Our children were happy and healthy. My wife was creatively decorating our home and making new friends. My private practice was thriving, and my tennis game was at its peak.

I had never been happier in my life. I knew who I was and where I was going. I felt committed to life and able to contribute much to my family, friends and profession.

Now I was unconscious. I knew no one and nothing about myself. I no longer enjoyed the security of an identity. My brain concussion left me with headaches as the only evidence that I was, in fact, alive.

For weeks, I struggled to find me. I felt depressed and valueless. I had no core of personality from which I could establish an identity. Gone was my humor and patience with children. Gone was my emotional connection to my wife and my memory of my patients. I had lost the first great gift life offers. I had lost a sense of me.

For the first time in my life, I recognized how enviable it is to be somebody—to truly feel unique and alive. I desperately needed my sense of identity. I wanted to scream, "I really can be fun and patient!" I felt desperate and lost without my personality.

As the weeks and months went by, I began to regain some of my memory. Tears came to my eyes many times when I realized I could still hold my wife and feel her love. The noise my children made began to excite me again as a reminder of how lucky I was to be alive and watch them grow up. Numerous phone calls and cards from people helped me remember the warmth of our friendships. It was as if I had experienced a sudden identity. And with my new identity came my commitment to live again.

Actually, I had merely found the old me again. After wandering for months in depression and severe memory loss, I felt new. I began to laugh and tease friends. I felt myself beginning to get comfortable with life, much like a guest who stays long enough in a home to feel like family. I was once again comfortable with my life because I had found my personality—my identity which determines my most natural style of presenting myself to the world.

Prior to the accident I had been working on this book. No experience could have been more timely than the accident. It convinced me of the incredible purpose our personalities play in our lives. It reminded me of my character strengths and limitations. It brought *me* back to *me*.

I am more sensitive today than I was before the accident. I had become too busy to play. I had become too busy to do the things I enjoyed most in my profession—time to call patients, send cards and listen to their triumphs. Now I take the time to go to lunch with friends and laugh until we're short on time, and must leave. Now I take the time to call my wife during the day just to say "I love you." Now I take the time to play baseball in the streets with my girls. Now I take the time to live and to love.

This close brush with death brought refreshing perspective to my life. All of us, in some way, experience our own crises. Perhaps these forced dilemmas afford us the luxury we might otherwise never afford ourselves—the sudden identity of who we really are and what we're really all about.

You, the reader, do not have to experience a serious accident to discover your own identity. You can be awakened to your sudden identity with a carefully designed test which will aid you in identifying your personality. Each personality will be fully explained with its strengths and limitations. You will be offered suggestions on how to develop your character in order to be your best self with your personality. Relationships between each personality style will also be discussed. You will be guided in assessing how to succeed in your various relationships at work, at home and with friends.

The Color Code is a book for us all to enjoy. You have a personality and character. It is not determined at birth what we will do with either of them. Unfortunately, many people simply grow old rather than ever growing up. This is your opportunity to understand the difference. It is my hope that *The Color Code* will be your guide to understanding and appreciating various personality types. Using the Color-Coded system described in the following chapters, you will learn how to improve your relationships, including the most important relationship of all—your relationship with yourself.

The Elements of Personality

Personality is innate.

Every child is born with a unique set of personality traits—often quite different from those of siblings. Ask any woman who has borne two or more children. She will attest to the fact that, while still in the womb, her children showed marked differences in their behavior. One may have "demanded" room to move. Another may have settled in quietly for the nine-month ride.

Everyone knows that no two sets of fingerprints are alike. How could we possibly believe that human personalities are any less "personal" than fingerprints?

There are professionals in the field of psychology who theorize that a child's personality is not completely formed until the age of five. Others go further—they say personality develops, slowly, through a life-long process of discovery and maturation. I disagree. I think some of my colleagues really mean "personal history" when they use the word personality.

I believe that each personality is complete at conception. It is present along with various genetically inherited traits, like hair color and blood type, although personality itself is not genetically linked. That is, it is not inherited from one's parents. Nor is it shaped by environment. At present, science has not discovered all the factors that determine our prenatal makeup. But this should not deter us from taking what we *do* know and using it to improve ourselves and our relationships.

Personality is a solid core of traits reflecting the unique essence of a particular human being. How does it arise? Social scientists have often tried to explain personality in terms of genetics or environmental influences, but without success. Such attempts merely limit our understanding of the true nature of personality. By confining themselves to the old genetics vs. environment argument (nature vs. nurture), such attempts to explain personality doom themselves to failure. Personality is not black and white. Personality is a kaleidoscope colored by many inexplicable twists and preferences. We can only understand personality—and ourselves—by opening our eyes to a whole new kind of understanding.

Even before we learned to mark time, humans were trying to learn what it was that made them tick. Greek legends abound with spellbinding stories of men and women who were changed by their interactions with one or more of the immortal gods. Early theorists tried to explain personality through such mythology, suggesting that people had unique strengths and limitations due to the influences of deities. Astrologers embraced the twelve signs of the zodiac as the determining factors in personality, substituting planetary power for the powers of the gods. Chinese tradition associated personality with the year a child was born.

Later theoreticians turned to the environment to explain personality differences. They categorized personalities according to four dominant aspects of nature—earth, air, fire and water. This theory of the elements provides us with an interesting starting point from which to proceed in our understanding of personality. It is simple, it is memorable, and it is rooted in fertile historical ground. I'll expand on this idea later. For the moment, the important thing to understand is that your personality is formed before you take your first breath.

Now let's explore the meaning of personality. What does it do? How does it affect our lives?

Personality is an interpretation of life.

Some people see the world through rose-colored glasses. Others see it through dark glasses. But we can't try on personalities the way we try on glasses. Personality is made of sterner stuff.

Your personality determines whether you are easily depressed, casual, formal, careful or carefree. It determines whether you are passive or assertive. Do you dash off at the last minute for an appointment, or always arrive with time to spare? Do you prefer deep, meaningful conversations or would you rather dance the night away? Are you most comfortable being entertained, or do you prefer to entertain others? Your personality is the key to how you react to these and all other situations. Your personality is more than just an "attitude." It is the *self* that causes you to act and react the way you do.

Personality is a code of behavior.

Personality is that core of thoughts and feelings inside you that tells you how to conduct yourself. It's a checklist of responses, based on innate values and strongly held beliefs. It directs your emotional as well as your rational reaction to *every life experience.* It even determines which type of reaction—emotional or rational—you're likely to fall back on in any given situation. Personality is an active process within each person's heart and mind that dictates how he or she feels, thinks and behaves.

Your personality watches over and guards you like a parent. It is what makes you different from everyone else, and so it is rigid and quite resistant to change. Personality protects itself. It does not easily venture out to experience or understand other types of personalities. It prefers the security and comfort of its own home. It accepts you—that is, itself—quite readily but is much less flexible with others. And, as sometimes happens between parents and children, it may give you problems from time to time. But let outsiders do or say something threatening and they are in *trouble!* Your personality, like a parent, reacts defensively and lashes out. Why? Because like anything that feels threatened, it is afraid.

Personality points each of us in a particular direction and makes us feel uncomfortable when we deviate from its assigned route. Without clear-cut personality traits to mark our paths through life, we would become lost. This is what personality fears most. The moment we stray from its prescribed plan, it makes us feel disoriented. We become mentally exhausted trying to deny or explain away unusual thought processes. We feel emotional fatigue and a vague sense of fear. We suffer spiritual pain that we cannot understand. We feel confused and overwhelmed by our inability to figure out how our thoughts and feelings have led us to seemingly irrational behavior. We feel mentally "upside-down" when we try to turn over a new leaf.

For each of us, the core of our personality—its type, the direction in which it points us—is vitally important in explaining us to ourselves. Without it, we would be truly lost. But it makes for rough going if we want to change, to grow. Each of us needs a personal code of behavior—a personality—but if we do not understand our personalities well enough to exert some control, we can never grow into healthier, happier human beings.

Personality is a mystery.

Sad, isn't it? For many people, their own personality is the greatest mystery of all. They are puzzled and frustrated when they do not understand the basis for their actions and reactions. However, few of us really know the reasons why we think and act as we do—perhaps none of us ever finds *complete* answers. Still, we can try. Trying to understand our personalities is the only way to grow. Step by step, bit by bit, we can gather enough knowledge about ourselves to begin to take control of our lives. I believe that life is the most exciting journey of all. It can be a better journey than you ever dreamed if you know where you've been and where you're going.

This book is designed to guide you in your journey of self-discovery. Knowledge is power. The knowledge you gain from this book will give you the power to change your behavior if you choose, and to understand the behavior of others.

Personality is a rainbow.

Let's return to the idea that the elements can be used as a metaphor for personality. Thousands of years ago, when the "known elements" were earth, air, fire and water, it was thought that there were also four distinct personality types. In this book I will borrow and expand upon the ancients' metaphor. In my Color Code, fire becomes the color Red, Blue reflects the earth, White represents water, and air is symbolized by Yellow.

Each color stands for a collection of traits-strengths and limitations. But far from being limited to explaining only individual personalities, this color symbolism also clarifies relationships between people and the impact that various personalities have on one another.

In order to understand the power of interactions between the four personality types, we can carry the nature analogy one step further. Earth without water is parched and desolate. And fire cannot exist without air. Symbolically, we see that each personality can define itself through its relationships with other personalities, rather than simply existing alone.

You should understand that the four primary personalities identified with the four colors are healthy and normal ones—the vast majority of people are basically healthy. These personality types are found in every culture in the world, in every age group, in every religion, race and sex. They belong to and describe everyone. They identify innate strengths as well as innate limitations. They color every action and reaction.

Of course, every person develops unique strengths and weaknesses—this makes for numerous variations within the four primary color groups. Also, some behavior patterns are not due to inherent personality at all, but instead reflect cultural biases—as, for instance, the submissive role played by women in some countries. Therefore, we must always look beyond culturally induced behavior to see the innate, natural personality of any individual.

Despite variations and exceptions, however, we can all identify best with only one of the personality colors. If we can each find our own personal color, learn its characteristics, and discover how to accentuate its strengths and work within its limitations, we will be better prepared to understand ourselves and cope with the everyday problems of life.

To help you accomplish this, a simple and enjoyable test appears in the next chapter. It will enable you to discover your personality color—first, so that you can understand and identify with the material in the rest of the book, and second, so you can learn to harness the strengths of your personality and enhance the rest of your life.

CHAPTER TWO

Personality Profile Test

Now it's time to discover your own personality type—your own "color." Perhaps you will learn things about yourself that you were not aware of, or find out why you have certain tendencies or reactions you could never understand. You will probably be able to identify the colors of some of your acquaintances as well. This will help you to understand them better, and point the way to more meaningful relationships.

It's unlikely that your color will prove to be a "pure" one—100% Red or Blue or White or Yellow. Nature isn't that simple. Instead, even those individuals with a strong affinity for one particular color will find it tinged with traces of others. When your test results reflect high scores in more than one personality area—that is, when two colors are almost equal in strength—you may at first find it difficult to identify the stronger one. Don't worry. As you read further, the motives and characteristics of each personality type will become clear and you will have no trouble determining your primary personality color.

As you seek your true identity, you may begin to see yourself differently—and more accurately. You will become aware of your many strengths. And though some of your suspicions about yourself may also be verified, you will be comforted in knowing that you are not alone—we all have a balance of strengths and weaknesses in our personality makeup. Don't be discouraged by any of the weaknesses you have. In the later chapters of the book, you will be motivated to turn limitations into assets. I will show you how.

In taking the Personality Profile Test, be as honest as you can. There's no point in deceiving yourself about who you really are. Dishonesty will only limit your knowledge of yourself and taint your relationships with others.

Here are some other suggestions that will make taking the test easier and will make your answers more accurate:

1. At first, mark the choices that come to you most readily. Skip the more difficult questions, but return to them later.

2. Do not hesitate to ask others for feedback—especially people who may not agree with you. Their opinions can help you balance your self-assessment.

3. Strive to choose answers which are most often typical of your thoughts and/or actions. Subconsciously, you may want to avoid identifying—or facing—the real you, but tough it out. Don't cheat yourself by prettying things up. The potential rewards for honesty are too great.

Now, enjoy the test. You are about to determine your true color.

Hartman Personality Profile

Directions: Mark an "X" by the one word or phrase that best describes what you are like *most of the time*. Choose only one response from each group. After you've finished question 30, total your scores for each letter.

Personality Strengths and Limitations

1. a) ___ opinionated
   b) ✓ nurturing
   c) ___ inventive
   d) ___ outgoing

2. a) ___ power-oriented
   b) ___ a perfectionist
   c) ✓ indecisive
   d) ___ self-centered

3. a) ___ dominant
   b) ✓ sympathetic
   c) ___ tolerant
   d) ___ enthusiastic

4. a) ___ self-serving
   b) ___ suspicious
   c) ___ unsure
   d) ✓ naive

5. a) ___ decisive
   b) ✓ loyal
   c) ___ contented
   d) ___ playful

6. a) ___ arrogant
   b) ✓ worry prone
   c) ___ silently stubborn
   d) ___ flighty

7. a) ___ assertive
   b) ___ reliable
   c) ✓ kind
   d) ___ sociable

8. a) ___ bossy
   b) ___ self-critical
   c) ✓ reluctant
   d) ___ a teaser

9. a) ___ action-oriented
   b) ___ analytical
   c) ✓ easygoing
   d) ___ carefree

10. a) ___ critical of others
    b) ✓ overly sensitive
    c) ___ shy
    d) ___ obnoxious

11. a) ___ determined
    b) ___ detail conscious
    c) ___ a good listener
    d) ___ a party person

12. a) ___ demanding
    b) ___ unforgiving
    c) ___ unmotivated
    d) ___ vain

13. a) ___ responsible
    b) ___ idealistic
    c) ___ considerate
    d) ___ happy

14. a) ___ impatient
    b) ___ moody
    c) ___ passive
    d) ___ impulsive

15. a) ___ strong-willed
    b) ___ respectful
    c) ___ patient
    d) ___ fun-loving

16. a) ___ argumentative
    b) ___ unrealistic
    c) ___ directionless
    d) ___ an interrupter

17. a) ___ independent
    b) ___ dependable
    c) ___ even-tempered
    d) ___ trusting

18. a) ___ aggressive
    b) ___ frequently depressed
    c) ___ ambivalent
    d) ___ forgetful

19. a) ___ powerful
    b) ___ deliberate
    c) ___ gentle
    d) ___ optimistic

20. a) ___ insensitive
    b) ___ judgmental
    c) ___ boring
    d) ___ undisciplined

21. a) ___ logical
    b) ___ emotional
    c) ___ agreeable
    d) ___ popular

22. a) ___ always right
    b) ___ guilt prone
    c) ___ unenthusiastic
    d) ___ uncommitted

23. a) ___ pragmatic
    b) ___ well-behaved
    c) ___ accepting
    d) ___ spontaneous

24. a) ___ merciless
    b) ___ thoughtful
    c) ___ uninvolved
    d) ___ a show-off

25. a) ___ task-oriented
    b) ___ sincere
    c) ___ diplomatic
    d) ___ lively

26. a) ___ tactless
    b) ___ hard to please
    c) ___ lazy
    d) ___ loud

27. a) ___ direct
    b) ___ creative
    c) ___ adaptable
    d) ___ a performer

28. a) ___ calculating
    b) ___ self-righteous
    c) ___ self-deprecating
    d) ✓ disorganized

29. a) ___ confident
    b) ___ disciplined
    c) ✓ pleasant
    d) ___ charismatic

30. a) ___ intimidating
    b) ✓ careful
    c) ___ unproductive
    d) ___ afraid to face facts

Strength and Limitation Totals

5 Total a's   4 Total b's   5 Total c's   1 Total d's

Enter your totals in the proper spaces. Now let's see if you respond the same way to the following situations as you did to groups of descriptive words. Again, pick only one answer, and record your totals for each letter at the end of the section.

Situations

31. If I applied for a job, a prospective employer would most likely hire me because I am:
    a. Driven, direct and delegating.
    b. Deliberate, accurate and reliable.
    c. Patient, adaptable and tactful.
    d. Funloving, spirited and casual.

32. When involved in an intimate relationship, if I feel threatened by my partner, I:
    a. Fight back with facts and anger.
    b. Cry, feel hurt and plan revenge.
    c. Become quiet, withdrawn and often hold anger until I blow up over some minor issue later.
    d. Distance myself and avoid further conflict.

33. For me, life is most meaningful when it:
    a. Is task-oriented and productive.
    b. Is filled with people and purpose.
    c. Is free of pressure and stress.
    d. Allows me to be playful, lighthearted and optimistic.

34. As a child, I was:
    a. Stubborn, bright and/or aggressive.
    b. Well-behaved, caring and/or depressed.
    c. Quiet, easy-going and/or shy.
    d. Too talkative, happy and/or playful.

35. As an adult, I am:
    a. Opinionated, determined and/or bossy.
    b. Responsible, honest and/or unforgiving.
    c. Accepting, contented and/or unmotivated.
    d. Charismatic, positive and/or obnoxious.

36. As a parent, I am:
    a. Demanding, quick-tempered and/or uncompromising.
    b. Concerned, sensitive and/or critical.
    c. Permissive, easily persuaded and/or often overwhelmed.
    d. Playful, casual and/or irresponsible.

37. In an argument with a friend I am most likely to be:
    a. Verbally stubborn about facts.
    b. Concerned about others' feelings and principles.
    c. Silently stubborn, uncomfortable and/or confused.
    d. Loud, uncomfortable and/or compromising.

38. If my friend was in trouble, I would be:
    a. Protective, resourceful and recommend solutions.
    b. Concerned, empathetic and loyal—regardless of the problem.
    c. Supportive, patient and a good listener.
    d. Nonjudgmental, optimistic and downplaying the seriousness of the situation.

39. When making decisions, I am:
    a. Assertive, articulate, and logical.
    b. Deliberate, precise, and cautious.
    c. Indecisive, timid and reluctant.
    d. Impulsive, uncommitted and inconsistent.

40. When I fail, I feel:
    a. Silently self-critical, yet verbally stubborn and defensive.
    b. Guilty, self-critical and vulnerable to depression—I dwell on it.
    c. Unsettled and fearful, but I keep it to myself.
    d. Embarrassed and nervous—seeking to escape the situation.

41. If someone crosses me:
    a. I am angered, and cunningly plan ways to get even quickly.
    b. I feel deeply hurt and find it almost impossible to forgive completely. Generally, getting even is not enough.
    c. I am silently hurt and plan to get even and/or completely avoid the other person.
    d. I want to avoid confrontation, consider the situation not important enough to bother with and/or seek other friends.

42. Work is:
    a. A most productive way to spend one's time.
    b. A healthy activity, which should be done right if it's to be done at all. Work should be done before one plays.
    c. A positive activity as long as it is something I enjoy and don't feel pressured to accomplish.
    d. A necessary evil, much less inviting than play.

43. In social situations, I am most often:
    a. Feared by others.
    b. Admired by others.
    c. Protected by others.
    d. Envied by others.

44. In a relationship, I am most concerned with being:
    a. Approved of and right.
    b. Understood, appreciated and intimate.
    c. Respected, tolerant and peaceful.
    d. Praised, having fun and feeling free.

45. To feel alive and positive, I seek:
    a. Adventure, leadership and lots of action.
    b. Security, creativity and purpose.

c. Acceptance and safety.

d. Excitement, playful productivity and the company of others.

Situations Totals

3 Total a's   2 Total b's   6 Total c's   1 Total d's

Now add your totals from number 1-30 to those from situation 31-45 to get grand totals. At this point, the four personality color types are assigned to each of the letters: Red for "a," Blue for "b," White for "c" and Yellow for "d."

GRAND TOTALS

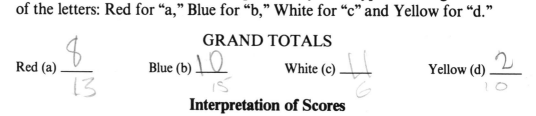

Red (a) 8
13

Blue (b) 10
15

White (c) 11
6

Yellow (d) 2
10

Interpretation of Scores

The letter with the greatest total reflects your natural personality. The number of responses from multiple columns suggests the amount of blend your personality represents. You have only one basic personality, but you may be a strong blend (behaviorally) of two personalities, depending on your responses. However, your motive (not your behavior) determines your primary personality (we'll get to that in Chapter Three).

If the totals from the word-choice section do not substantially agree with the totals from the situations section, you will find further guidance in later chapters on the various colors and their motives.

Welcome Back!

How does it feel to have a new identity, and immediate membership in an elite group of people bearing your color? Even allowing for your uniqueness, there is a strong bond of similarity between you and everyone who shares your distinct color characteristics.

You must consider this color profile as a guide, not a directive engraved in stone. Few people are completely represented by just one personality type. Your color reflects your primary personality, but, like most people, you are probably a mixture of types. The degree to which you have marked responses other than those of your main color reflects this. You are, however, *always* predominantly one color, one personality.

As a result of taking the Personality Profile Test, you have discovered the first important truth about yourself. You are either a *purist* (predominantly one color, totalling 30 or more responses to a single letter) or a *mixed personality* (two or more colors representing almost equal totals).

Suddenly, you have a new identity—perhaps an unexpected one. You did not choose it, study for it, or acquire it through conscious effort. Nor can your parents claim genetic responsibility for it. Your personality is uniquely and refreshingly *you*.

Mixed Colors

While purists find it easy to relate to examples that reflect primary colors, mixed-color personalities do not. They are more complex. The characteristics of their behavior and their motives are harder to pin down.

The most difficult color combination is Red and Blue. If you are strong in both categories, you will often find yourself stepping on someone's toes to get a task completed (Red), but feeling guilty afterward for making that person unhappy (Blue). The chapter on motives will help you understand your constant struggle between seeking power and searching for intimacy in relationships.

Red-White combinations are difficult to read because they can be aggressive and determined one minute (Red), then quietly passive the next (White). If you fit this category, your guiding motive is power or peace rather than intimacy, which spares you the intense struggle of the Red-Blue combination. You are likely to be misunderstood because your behavior is inconsistent, and you don't easily allow others to figure you out.

If you're a Red-Yellow, you are a natural leader and find yourself in a comfortable blend. The Red dynamically directs your life, while the Yellow charismatically invites others to enjoy your friendship.

If you're a Blue-White combination, you are comfortable. You express yourself softly and sincerely. Your personality is easy to read. People find you determined, yet flexible. You are someone with whom almost anyone can get along.

Blue-Yellows are fun to tease. I call them my dual personalities, because they can be footloose and carefree one minute then suddenly turn very serious the next. They may pack the neighborhood kids in the van and race to the beach for a day of sun and fun. But once there, they'll start to worry about all the things they should be doing at home. They are intimacy-based and have no strong desire for power in their relationships.

If White and Yellow are your two strong colors, you possess the best people skills of all the personalities. You are relaxed and usually take the path of least resistance. You do not experience much conflict between your colors, despite the different motives represented by each. You are comfortable with your blend and present an inviting atmosphere to those around you.

Ultimately—whoever *you* are—you are driven by one basic personality. You must find it even though it may be concealed in a mix of two or more colors. All healthy individuals have just *one* primary personality; therefore it is essential that you determine your basic color. A person with one watch knows the time, but a person with two or more is never sure.

You will find clues to your primary personality—no matter how much of a blend you may be—in the following chapter on motives. As you read, remember that you should always defer to your natural personality strength. *Do what comes naturally.* That is the straightest path to inner peace.

Now let's continue—as Reds, Blues, Whites and Yellows. We will begin by identifying and exploring the needs, desires and motives of each of the colors in the complex and fascinating rainbow of personalities.

CHAPTER THREE

Color-Coded Motives

You have just taken a test that has revealed your personality color.

The test listed many *behaviors*. Behaviors are determined by *needs* and *wants*. For example, if a Red needs to be right, his or her behavior is likely to be opinionated. And if a Red wants a leadership position, his or her behavior is likely to be assertive and/or bossy.

Many of us are familiar with the Peanuts cartoon strip that features Lucy, a Red child who *needs* to be right and *wants* leadership. As a result, her behavior is dominant and bossy ("crabby" in Charlie Brown's terminology). Her needs and wants direct her behavior.

Just as behavior is directed by needs and wants, needs and wants are determined by *motives*. Motives are our innermost reasons. They explain *why* we think and behave as we do. They are the driving force behind our personalities. Motives are to our personalities what engines are to our cars.

Motives are the principle means of identifying a personality color.

Each color stands for one particularly strong motive. Red is for power. Blue is for intimacy. White is for peace. Yellow is for fun. Let's take another look at Lucy. Her primary color, Red, is identified with the *power* motive, which creates a need to be right and a desire for leadership. Consequently, she behaves in a dominant and bossy manner.

I am reminded of a White male patient of mine. (Remember: "White" is his personality color, not necessarily his race. When it comes to race, we should all be color-blind.) For five years, this patient carried on an affair with a woman he loved, while staying in a marriage that was based solely on social obligations and pressures. There was no love or companionship in his marriage. Many other men might have moved out, divorced their wives, and gone off with the other woman. But this man, a White personality, had peace as his primary motive. He didn't want to rock the boat. He wouldn't—or couldn't—confront his wife. He had great need to feel good inside, and a confrontation would have been painful. He sought to please both himself (by having an affair) and others (by staying married to his wife). At this point, his motives, needs, and wants were pulling him in different directions. It is no surprise then, that an unhealthy behavior pattern followed. He was unhappy, and he made those around him unhappy, too.

Motives, needs and wants are neither good nor bad. They are neutral. They become healthy or unhealthy depending on how they relate to the truth. (I will discuss truth in more depth in Chapter Eight.)

The White motive of peace can be healthy if it benefits everyone involved. In the case of the married man, the White motive of peace was selfish. His unwillingness to be honest with his wife and face the consequences of his behavior kept her from finding someone else to love. It kept his girlfriend from enjoying the true intimacy that would have come from sharing his warmth and companionship on a full-time basis. And it kept him from developing his character and pursuing his needs and wants in any positive way. His motive—peace—was neutral, but his actions were unhealthy, dishonest and selfish. He made a mess of his life and the lives of everyone involved with him.

My White patient's story has a happy ending. He learned to develop his character and clean up his motives. He scraped up enough courage to be honest with his wife. He moved into an apartment of his own—which was difficult and uncomfortable, especially for a comfort-loving White personality—and remained alone until he could decide which woman to live with. Ultimately, he chose his girlfriend. As difficult as this process was, it freed all concerned to pursue healthy and fulfilling lives. His decision was the first step in getting his motives in line with the realities of his life.

This man hit upon the key to success, no matter what the personality color. He examined his motives, realized what hardship he was creating in pursuing them in an unhealthy way, and put them in a new, positive and healthy perspective. Being White, he still desired peace, but he recognized that he could never find real peace until he faced the truth about his behavior. By facing the truth, he defied his innate personality limitations (passiveness, indecisiveness and the need to keep peace at all costs), and developed a healthy sense of his own character. He eventually achieved tremendous success in all his personal relationships—because of his new willingness to align his motives, needs, wants and behaviors with truth.

This brief example illustrates the strengths and weaknesses of the White personality, but each color has its own unique set of needs, wants and behavior patterns, all sparked by a unique set of motives. Now that you know your own personality color, what are *your* particular motives, needs and wants? What does *your* true color reveal about you?

REDS

Reds are hungry for power.

Simply stated, Reds want their own way. If they have been raised in environments where they were able to manipulate their parents and siblings, they become difficult to manage as they get older. When they have gotten their way for too long, Reds find it almost impossible to relinquish their power and freedom when they meet authorities in society (teachers, bosses, police, clergy, military officers) who refuse to grant them the total control they demand.

Reds want to be productive.

Reds like to work—in school, in their careers and in their relationships. Just don't expect them to attach the same importance to things other people care about—like other people's schooling, careers and marriages. But give them a reason to produce, and watch them take off. Reds like to get the job done. They are often workaholics. They will, however, resist being forced to do anything that doesn't interest them.

Reds want to look good to others.

Reds need to appear knowledgeable. They crave approval from others for their intelligence and insight. They want to be respected even more than they want to be loved. They want to be admired for their logical, practical minds. When you deal with a Red, be precise and factual. Reds are unmoved by tears and other displays of "weakness."

Red shouldn't be taken too seriously.

Reds are often just stating the facts as they see them, despite their antagonistic demeanor. They seldom say "in my opinion" before stating their opinions. I have seen too many Blues, Whites and Yellows become greatly concerned over issues raised by Reds, only to discover later that the Reds were simply interested in debating. Reds enjoy a good power play. But once you get emotionally involved arguing issues, you may be disappointed and frustrated to find that a Red is no longer interested.

Reds seek leadership opportunities.

Despite the rigidity of the military, many young Red men and women select it as a career in order to experience leadership. Reds are often called "control freaks." They like to be in the driver's seat. Red children are often frustrated in school because teachers (often Blue personalities) won't let them take charge. If a Red can get the upper hand, he or she will. Reds are willing to pay any price in order for an opportunity to lead.

BLUES

Blues are motivated by altruism.

Blues love to do nice things for others. They look for opportunities to give up something in order to bring another person happiness. Selflessness rather than selfishness is their guiding philosophy. Many Blues are uncomfortable doing things solely for themselves. They hold doors open for people, offer rides when someone's car breaks down, contribute to charity, even devote their entire lives to helping others.

Blues crave intimacy.

More than anything else, Blues want to love and be loved. A Blue will sacrifice a successful career to improve an important relationship. Once considered a female characteristic, this nurturing is more accurately understood as a Blue personality trait.

Blues are gratified when they are listened to, when they feel understood and appreciated. They are notorious for revealing their inadequacies because they value being known and understood so much. In the eyes of a Blue, being vulnerable is small price to pay for the chance to be close. Blues may have their hearts broken more than most people, but they also spend much more time in love.

Blues need to be loved.

With Blues, a simple pat on the back will not suffice. Blues expend such great effort in making the world a better place that sometimes they need to be told how wonderful they are. They need to be thanked and specifically remembered for their good deeds. They need sincere gratitude. They delight in being remembered on birthdays and other special days, especially if the remembrance is personal—a homemade anniversary card, a welcome home party, a special day that isn't on the calendar. Blues need tender loving care.

Blues are directed by a strong moral conscience.

Blues are motivated to behave in a proper, appropriate manner. They have a moral code that guides them in their decision making, their value judgments, even their leisure time. Blues enjoy being "good." Of all the personality colors, Blues come equipped with the strongest sense of integrity. A Blue would rather lose than cheat. Blues are trustworthy. Blues are the people who should be in positions of power, but seldom are.

WHITES

Whites are motivated by peace.

Whites will do almost anything to avoid confrontation. They like to flow through life without hassle or discomfort. *Feeling* good is even more important to them than *being* good.

Whites need kindness.

While Whites respond beautifully to thoughtfulness and amiability, they have a strong, silent stubbornness that surfaces when they are treated unkindly. They resent being scolded. They dislike harsh words. They open up instantly to people who are kind, but Whites recoil from those who are hostile. They are motivated by kindness—and can't understand why other people are unkind.

Whites like to keep a low profile.

Whites enjoy their quiet independence. What appears to some people as quiet desperation can show itself to be bullheadedness. Those who misinterpret the peace-loving nature of a White as an invitation to be demanding and bossy will soon meet a wall of passive resistance. Whites are tougher than people think.

Whites like to be asked their opinions. They won't volunteer them. They value the respect of others, but they rarely go out of their way to seek it. They need to be coaxed to talk about their skills, hobbies and interests.

Whites are independent.

Unlike Reds, who want to control others, Whites seek only to avoid being controlled. They simply refuse to be under another's thumb, especially when treated without the respect they feel they deserve. Whites want to do things their own way, in their own time. They don't ask much of others, and resent it when others demand things from them. They often comply with unreasonable demands—just to keep peace. They will only express their anger and frustration when they can no longer stand being bossed around. Whites don't like to be pushed, and they can be fearsome when they finally "blow up."

Whites are motivated by other people's desires.

Whites are open to the recommendations of others on ways to resolve any and all situations. White executives value new management ideas from employees. White children welcome help—they are eager students. Whites make agreeable dates. They are interested in making sure the other person has a good time, and are willing to do whatever the other person wants. Whites, however, want suggestions—not demands.

YELLOWS

Yellows value play.

Yellows consider life to be a party. And they're hosting. One father (Blue) was disappointed when his son (Yellow) preferred spending time with friends instead of with him. I reminded the father that his son was motivated by fun, and suggested that he should try to come up with activities that his son felt were exciting. It was the "better offer" principle—and it worked. Yellows just want to have fun.

Yellows welcome praise.

Yellows need to be noticed. Nothing improves a relationship with a Yellow more than praise. Yellows need to know they are valued and approved of. Yellows often act as though they have the world by the tail, but they do have their fears and frustrations—which they rarely confide until they know they are loved. Love is most effectively given to Yellows through praise.

Yellows need intimacy.

Yellows often appear so nonchalant that people think they don't care about anything. Nothing could be further from the truth. Yellows need a great deal of attention. They need to be stroked. Yellows enjoy touching. To them, physical contact is the most direct, most intimate connection.

Yellows want to be popular.

Yellows like to be at center stage. Socially looking good is very important to them. Friendships command a high priority in their lives because popularity answers one of their basic needs—the need for approval. Yellows are highly verbal. They relish good conversation. But they can also go with the flow— they can chit-chat superficially with the best of them.

Yellows like action.

Easily bored, Yellows seek adventure. They can never sit still for long. They choose friends who, like them, refuse to allow the "boring details" to get in the way of the most important thing in life—play.

Now that you are familiar with the motives, needs, wants and behaviors of each personality color, let's get an overview of the basics.

Personality Overview

	RED	BLUE	WHITE	YELLOW
MOTIVE	Power	Intimacy	Peace	Fun
NEEDS	To look good (academically)	To be good (morally)	To feel good (inside)	To look good (socially)
	To be right	To be understood	To be understood	To be popular

Personality Overview (continued)

	RED	BLUE	WHITE	YELLOW
NEEDS	To be respected	To be appreciated	To be respected	To be praised
	Approval	Acceptance	Acceptance	Approval
WANTS	To hide insecurities (tightly)	To reveal insecurities	To reveal insecurities	To hide insecurities (loosely)
	To please self	To please others	To please others	To be noticed
	Leadership	Autonomy	Protection	Freedom
	Challenging adventure	Security	Contentment	Playful adventure

Having identified all four personalities and the motives behind them, we will continue, in the following chapters, to examine the strengths and limitations of each personality color. Remember that all of the characteristics of *your* primary color may not reflect your own personality. But the motives, needs and wants behind those characteristics do influence you.

You will notice that occasionally the same characteristics appear in two different personalities. This is due to the fact that there are similarities as well as differences between the colors. Generally, however, you will find one color that fits your behavior better than any other.

As you identify your strengths, you can get acquainted with your limitations at the same time. Limitations are nothing to be afraid of. Each color has much to learn from the others. But we are most effective in understanding other people when we see them whole—treating them as complete personalities rather than focusing on either their strengths or limitations.

Reading about one's limitations can be painful. It can be very difficult to acknowledge areas in which we are weak. (Especially you Reds!) We prefer to shield ourselves from that information. So prepare yourself for a little discomfort. "It will only hurt for a minute," as the doctor says. Take stock in the fact that the cure is better than the disease. And in this case, the cure is knowledge. The best thing about limitations is that, once understood, they can be turned into strengths.

CHAPTER FOUR

Reds: The Power Wielders

Active and Productive

The Red personality moves forcefully through life. As Helen Keller said, "Life is either a daring adventure or nothing at all." Reds are highly committed to causes and find themselves determined to accomplish whatever life places before them. In fact, they seek challenges and with rare exception they rise to the occasion. As a result of their tenacious nature, Reds often are successful. Their success comes primarily from business and task-oriented activities while the Blues, for example, usually experience their success with deep interpersonal relationships or in highly creative fields. Reds seek action and results. They crave productivity. They measure their success by how much (versus how well) they accomplish. Simply stated, Reds get things done.

Insensitive and Selfish

Reds are so clearly defined that one finds it difficult to believe they would not instantly recognize the color of their personality. Many do. But often the most critical stumbling block for Red individuals in identifying themselves is *denial*. Reds are proud and known to parade their values and opinions in the faces of all others. They can present themselves in a distant and insensitive manner. A mother had promised to take her Red teen-aged daughter to the library in order to study for a school report. Prior to their departure, the mother and father engaged in a traumatic verbal conflict and the father threatened divorce. The daughter witnessed the entire one hour ordeal. The mother was devastated and crying uncontrollably when her daughter said, matter-of-factly, "Mom, will we still be able to get to the library before it closes tonight?!" Only Reds can be so insensitive to the feelings of others! This weakness may explain why Reds are more successful at developing and promoting ideas, events, and business ventures than quality relationships.

"King of the Jungle"

Considering their productive and tenacious natures, it is no wonder Reds exude incredible self-confidence. They appear strong and certain of themselves. As such, few people are willing to confront them. This strength bestows on them the most feared title of all personalities, "King of the Jungle." When people seek advice and direction they find Reds are most helpful. Reds have a sense of what is right and often express themselves in a manner few people can logically refute. Many Reds are notably intelligent and skilled in making good decisions. Subsequently, others choose to follow. And why not? When you find a good doctor, why seek another? It is their uncanny and enviable ability of being right so often that influences others to place them in leadership positions. It is the Red's natural gift and desire to lead that drives them to select opportunities of advancement to the top of many organizations, businesses and other affiliations.

Perhaps the most intriguing complexity of Red's apparent self-confidence AND frustrating arrogance lies in their deep insecurity. They seek the very acceptance and understanding they often refuse to give others. However, this need is placed so deeply within their hearts where they can skillfully protect it, that it is often well hidden from their rational mind's eye. Deferring to their logic, they refuse to acknowledge emotional vulnerability. As youths, while yet somewhat sensitive to emotions, their insecurities are more clearly viewed. Unfortunately, with age and increased skill at logic, they usually keep their deep emotional insecurities adeptly disguised from others. With time, they often lose an accurate perspective and actually believe they have no need for emotion. The irony is that in order for Reds to experience a full and intimate life, they must expose themselves to perhaps their greatest fear—their emotional insecurity and need to be loved and accepted.

Demanding and Critical

Reds are highly critical of others. Most Reds are verbally critical while others remain quietly dissatisfied with other's performance in life. They are rather impatient with human inadequacy and feel nothing short of efficiency should be tolerated. While Reds are not as perfectionistic as Blues (thank our lucky stars), they do want a job done right and expediently. They have no tolerance for mental dullness, lack of common sense or being unprepared. They expect results and spare little time reminding others of their expectations. They can be highly biased and reactionary in their judgments of others. The irony lies in how emotionally based this behavior is, when one realizes the logical rigidity which permeates the thinking and behavior of most Reds.

Insecure

Reds can bury their own personal insecurities deep enough so as to not consciously feel the pain of their exposure. Subsequently, they are often insensitive to the raw nerves they touch in others who are less willing (or able) to hide their vulnerability. Reds seriously mean no harm to the individual as long as the Red's productivity is enhanced and they are proved to be right. Reds have little sympathy for impeding progress, regardless of the source—be it employees, children, spouses, friends, or even God.

Must be Right

Driven by their need to hide emotional insecurities, they demand to be right. They do not ask whether they are perceived by others as right. They simply state that they are right one hundred percent of the time. Even after evidence dictates that Reds are inaccurate, they often brush their error aside as a misunderstanding or misinterpretation. A family was looking for an office building but didn't know the exact address. One teen-ager remarked, "I think it's near the corner of Moody and Lincoln." Her Red older sister, Ginny, replied, "Oh, no it's not. It couldn't be there. I know *all* the buildings over there." Ginny was driving and ignored the suggestion. One hour later, after several telephone calls, they pulled up in front of the office building right on the corner of Moody and Lincoln. When they arrived home, the mother suggested that in the future perhaps *all* suggestions should be entertained with an open mind. To this Ginny scoffed, "I know she didn't say Moody and Lincoln. She must have said somewhere else. After all, I'm the one who finally found it, didn't I?!!!"

Competitive and Bold

Reds are daring and bold—both traits luring them away from the business world or home duties to excel in adventures such as mountain climbing, hang gliding or building their own home. However, Reds can also find great excitement in promoting an innovative concept or gaining the competitive edge in the business world. Combining their brave and competitive strengths, Reds are bold within organizational structures as well as personal settings.

In business, at home or with friends and hobbies, Reds are certain to get their share of the pie. Simply stated, they are typically selfish. They know what they want and often control events and people in order to achieve it. They are not concerned much with guilt feelings or compassion for others. Ironically, very insecure Reds seek attention and make certain that whatever inconvenience they must endure (i.e., illnesses or accidents) is shared by others in their life.

Tenacious and Taxing

Whether ill or in good health, Reds are a taxing personality. They are so tenacious and bossy that they begin to wear you down rather rapidly. Reds remind me of house guests who want the household schedule adapted to *their* personal schedule. After a short period of time with this overbearing personality, a change and breath of fresh air is not only welcome—it's necessary.

In their leadership, Reds can also be bossy. They often expect subordinates to remember their place in the pecking order and respond accordingly. They are often hard to work for or live with because they order others around with little regard for established schedules, family commitments, or professional concerns. If they are challenged they often become aggressive due to their intimidating nature and arrogant attitude. Whether they maintain a position of leader or follower, Reds are often inclined to make their point aggressively to whomever crosses their path. They are not shamed by public awareness of their concern. Without much tact, they relentlessly pursue elements in their life which need attention whether it be a misplaced hotel accommodation or a child's unacceptable report card. Aggression makes a point without concern for other individual's feelings. Unhealthy Reds are typically aggressive.

Assertive and Determined

On the other hand, positive assertion flows as easily to the healthy Red personality as water falls from a duck's back. They need no coaxing to establish their position in any situation. "Knowing" that they are right, helps convince Reds of their position while intimidating the other parties. Business groups are *always* enhanced by the presence of healthy Reds. Reds speak their minds directly and honestly regardless of their popularity.

They are very strong-willed and determined. Reds take firm stands and expect others to follow. Others often do follow when Reds present themselves and their ideas with clean motives. However, this same strength of determination can also be experienced as a limitation when Reds are disagreeable or argumentative.

Disagreeable

Disagreeable is a word that comes to mind when pondering Red limitations. Whether it is for the sake of maintaining the fine art of debate, or a driving need to convert the world to their beliefs, Reds can be quite opinionated and stubborn on most topics ranging from how to pay a bill (by cash, check or credit card) to meeting deadlines ("I don't care if I don't need it by Wednesday. You still need to complete it because I told you to!")

Complementing this disagreeable nature and their logical minds, Reds often enjoy verbal argumentation. They seem comfortable with this style of ideas, conflict and verbal expression. It requires very little for a Red to confront another person. Verbally, it is so routine that they rarely even recognize the conflict they created at all.

Reds are not natural conversationalists. They are natural lecturers. Listening and empathy are often limited tools of the Red personality. These limitations cause many Reds to experience loneliness. They rarely admit their loneliness. They often blame it on others (i.e., "my husband left me in this mess without a friend in the world"—spoken by a Red woman ten years after their divorce. Or "If people were only more educated or intelligent they could appreciate me.")

Resourceful and Self-Reliant

Reds often challenge those in authority and *successfully* control their own destiny. One of the positive reasons they can challenge authority and effectively maintain their independent natures is their resourcefulness and self-reliance. If I was ever caught in an emergency or distressing situation, I would most prefer to be in the company of a Red personality. They eat, sleep and breathe action. No situation will get the best of them until they have exhausted every possibility to remedy the problem. They simply don't give up easily. They are rarely intimidated or threatened by life's obstacles. They have an inner competitive sense and whatever or whomever sets themselves up as the opponent (whether it be an earthquake or mother-in-law) will not find an easy victory.

Relentless and Impatient

If you need an agent, a fundraising chairperson or a political ally, advertise for the Red personality characteristics. Nobody promotes like a Red. I have already alluded to their bold, assertive, and competitive nature. They are also pragmatic. Rather than concerning themselves with the frills, they get at the heart of problems and quickly demand a resolution.

Reds throw themselves into causes. If they feel you have something worthwhile to offer, they will gladly give their efforts to assist you. Upon discovering a child's dancing talents, Red parents drive long distances and provide financial assistance to see their child succeed. (In fact, this book would most likely never have seen its current form if it were not for the assistance of three close Red friends. Two gave me the confidence to write with numerous suggestions, time and support. The other met me for early morning breakfasts, demanding to read a new chapter every time we met. When I cancelled our first breakfast, my friend called me at 11:00 p.m. the night before our scheduled breakfast and asked if I was cancelling because I hadn't completed my "homework." She was right. I was sliding and needed her encouragement.)

Reds are relentless in their commitment to causes they believe in. They are as comfortable promoting others as they are themselves when they are committed to a concept. When converted to a concept, Reds know no equal. They are difficult to convince but equally difficult to restrain once converted.

Reds usually pursue whatever they want (whether it is healthy or unhealthy) until they have it. Red infants demand to be held *immediately* upon request (crying). Red salespeople not only demand that you listen but also require you to answer silly questions, (i.e., "Now really, Mrs. Meriweather, wouldn't you like to drive a new Cadillac rather than the old one your friends have seen you drive for years?!"). They want everyone to respond when and how they determine is appropriate. They struggle with impatience. They can't wait for others to "grow up" and behave like Reds know they ought to behave. Red parents often demand respect rather than concern themselves with earning it. Red employers can't tolerate indecisiveness or poor productivity. One of their gravest errors in leadership style is impatience. They typically step in too quickly and often too harshly as well.

Calculating and Manipulative

Reds are often calculating and manipulative in order to control lives and produce results. Reds are not flippant—casually tossing their lives in the air and hoping for a favorable wind. They create their own wind and attempt to force life to blow in their direction.

I have seen the lives of close friends temporarily destroyed by the shrewd manipulation of an unhealthy Red personality. As a young professional, I worked for a drug prevention program. Many of my colleagues were former drug users and had confided in our boss many of the events, feelings and fears they were struggling with in their pursuit of a drug-free life. He hired these individuals knowing their personal life histories and then used this knowledge to back them down when they inquired about raises, promotions or other work-related expectations which he disliked.

Comments like, *"Now* I understand why your father threw you out of the house. Were you this defiant when *he* asked small favors of you?" or "You still expect something else to make you happy—first drugs, and now more money," were common in staff or individual meetings with this director.

As business people, they can often be brilliant and brutal in one fell swoop. Unfortunately, this calculating mind reduces true intimacy to an impractical notion as well as a highly unlikely probability. One Red patient eventually lost the woman of his dreams because he kept postponing their marriage in order to get the right timing for the best tax break. Intimacy requires equality and a competitive Red with a calculating mind doesn't often find equality to be a worthy ambition.

Lack Intimacy Orientation

Without question, the greatest deterrent to a Red's success in experiencing a quality lifestyle lies in their inability to be intimate with other people. They are so determined and productive that their lack of intimacy is often ignored or denied as a significant concern. Unless corrected, it does eventually relegate Reds to a supervisory "caretaker of humanity" role, as opposed to an intimate "member of the human team."

Reds probably watch more television and put in overtime at work more than any other personality. Unfortunately, this also diverts them from ever having to face the issue of intimacy in relationships. They rarely have hobbies (like the Blues and Whites) or friends (like the Yellows). They are lost without their career or family. On a recent river rafting trip a Red could hardly wait three hours to find a phone so he could call his wife and see how she was doing. It sounds all very romantic but the reality was that he had not been away from her in ten years of marriage and despite being with close friends he felt lost and uncomfortable without her at his side. Truth is, he is rarely *with* her even when he is at home. Rather, he is constantly working on a book or writing an article. He rarely just sits with her. But he *needs* her. And needing his affection, she plays along with his "attentive" phone calls, acting as if his sun rises and sets with her.

Reds are often the first to remind you they are eager to leave home and be out on their own at eighteen years of age. They are also the first to come home (whether physically or emotionally) and seek the comfort of a loving and caring family. Some Reds will milk every last ounce of sympathy their sickness can muster up, (especially Red men). Other Reds hide their pain and discomfort. These behaviors are dishonest and selfish. They do not lead to genuine intimacy. Rather, they most often leave a Red individual skeptical and lonely.

This emptiness often creates a very angry individual who *feels* very deeply their powerlessness to demand quality relationships. One forty year old male patient told me he had never learned to love. He realized it through our sessions working with his son. One session he wept, "I finally woke up at forty and realized I did not know the slightest thing about living or loving." This anger comes from the frustration of Reds wanting to *control* rather than *share* their destiny and with Reds it lies at the very base of their insecurities. They want a loving relationship but find they are powerless to control the process. As a result, many abandon their wants for a more controlled lifestyle.

Red Limitations

Reds are a myriad of dynamic limitations. They are not subtle and undefined. Reds are actually easily detected and understood. They can be difficult to live and work with unless they get their way. Reds are often taxing and demanding. They will argue at the "drop of a hat." Their selfish nature is a constant reminder to other personalities that Reds will always consider themselves number one. They are often insensitive and arrogant which creates a distance and distrust. Intimacy is, perhaps, their least developed skill. They can find themselves to be lonely due to their critical and disagreeable nature. They argue from logic and are capable of manipulating with constant mind calculation. Highly verbal individuals, Reds often attack others and intimidate inadequate human beings. They are particularly guilty of denial ("Who, me?!") They are often surprised to find out that others may see them in a negative light, but feel finding fault with others to be an essential part of their daily routine. Their tactless and stubborn behavior tends to expose a frustrated individual who blooms with positions of power and control and yet shrinks from social life when their leadership opportunities run dry. Always processing a new thought in their mind, these often brilliant individuals must be constantly aware of their limitations in order to avoid sabotaging themselves from experiencing a quality life.

Red Strengths

Healthy Reds are the life blood of humanity. They are the movers and shakers of society. They are known for their dominant nature. They are the powerful leaders and responsible delegators. Red personalities can be an asset to any organization. They enjoy competition and challenges. They call easily upon their inner core for self-motivation and direction.

They focus precisely when setting goals and tenaciously assert their rights (and the rights of any organization, person, or cause they value). They value productivity and success and willingly pay the price for both. They enjoy organizational teamwork as well as individualism. Reds promote most aspects of life with self-confidence and tenacity. They are constant reminders of the power derived from rational thinking and assertive communication. They are the standard we use to measure our intellectual prowess. They model those leadership skills we seek to emulate. Reds represent the fire espoused by early theorists in the nature theory. Their lights continue to burn brightly as a beacon of strength and productivity, warming and reassuring us with their resourceful and protective nature.

Red Strengths

AS AN INDIVIDUAL

- excels with logical thinking
- committed to a productive lifestyle
- dynamic and direct
- thrives on independence
- natural leader
- highly resourceful (strong survivor)
- creative in crises

AS A COMMUNICATOR

- operates in a very logical, sensible manner
- direct and honest with opinions
- communicates thoughts well in verbal conversation
- directs the conversation in a productive, pragmatic way
- tells others where they stand in a relationship

AS A GOAL SETTER

- natural goal setter—set goals comfortably and confidently
- maintains strong sense of perspective (sees the whole picture)
- highly disciplined
- highly productive with follow through
- makes decisions quickly and easily

AS A CAREER PERSON

- thrives in leadership positions
- comfortable with power (as long as he or she has it)
- strong goal orientation (wants to move up the ladder)
- excellent organizer
- delegates superbly
- quick to make decisions and handles responsibilities well
- self-motivated
- thrives on competition
- dynamic and assertive career lifestyle

- highly task-oriented and efficient
- confident with ability to achieve
- trusts one's business instincts—difficult to discourage

AS A PARENT

- excellent decision maker
- unquestioned as leader in home
- assumes responsibility for protecting family
- excellent provider
- quick with good advice and direction
- promotes group cohesiveness or comfortable being alone
- promotes children's activities

AS A CHILD

- communicates what he or she is thinking
- strong sense of independence
- willing to risk and try new experiences
- takes charge of situation when parents are gone
- capable of bouncing back in negative environment
- maintains the power to turn a poor situation around
- believes in self—maintains high self-esteem
- highly verbal

AS A FRIEND

- direct and quick with suggestions
- great in emergencies or disasters
- promotes group activities
- engages in conflict comfortably and directly
- productive in solving dilemmas

AS A COMMITTED COMPANION

- highly protective of companion
- loyal to the relationship
- promotes interesting experiences
- takes primary responsibility for financial needs

- reliable and dependable
- initiates interaction and activities

CAREERS MOST LIKELY TO ATTRACT REDS

Administrator	Lawyer	Building Contractor
Police Officer	Medical Doctor	Sales
Military Officer	Indian Chief	Marketing
Politician	Realtor	Clergy (Minister)
Entrepreneur	Film Critic	School Superintendant

Note: Reds are most often frustrated if they are not at the top of the career ladder.

All personality types can be found in every occupation due to the numerous variables considered in career choice.

PERSONALITIES WHO APPEAR TO BE POSITIVE REDS

Margaret Thatcher	Katharine Hepburn	John Wayne

RED NATIONS

U.S.S.R.	Japan	Germany

Red Limitations

AS AN INDIVIDUAL

- generally seeks to serve self (what's in it for me?)
- promotes turmoil and conflict with some personal goal to be gained
- rationalizes and denies personal behavior
- always right
- cannot relax and feel comfortable without producing something
- often arrogant and defiant of authority
- inconsiderate of other's feeling (selfish)
- out of touch with personal feelings
- won't share inadequacies for fear of losing power and control

AS A COMMUNICATOR

- unemotional and detached from feelings
- insensitive and tactless
- unappreciative of detail and beauty
- bored with insignificant "idle chatter"
- poor insight into others due to lack of emotional perspective
- intuition is jaded by personal insecurities and judgments
- harsh and judgmental
- lacks ability to share self intimately

AS A GOAL SETTER

- impatient with self in completing goals
- too rigid with expectations of his or her destiny
- lives life on paper rather than with people
- promotes quantity rather than quality
- angered easily if goals aren't achieved or become blocked
- blames others for personal misfortunes

AS A CAREER PERSON

- seeks power to control others
- refuses to relax—drives self and others
- dislikes being told what to do
- may be insensitive to others in order to get ahead in business
- makes decisions too quickly
- doesn't often think the problem through or consult others for advice
- not concerned with people as much as task completion
- requires other's loyalty and obedience
- authoritarian and uncompromising
- critical of others and slow to give compliments
- often too competitive to enjoy the competition

AS A PARENT

- expects high performance without offering assistance
- wants strict obedience

- requires loyalty from family at all costs
- unfeeling and insensitive to children's fears and concerns
- requires the final say on important decisions
- detached from children—doesn't share self emotionally
- does not tolerate deviations from set expectations
- establishes harsh and limiting boundaries
- poor listener
- impatient with play and other non-essential trivia
- lacks insight into children's emotional needs
- difficult to please—remains unimpressed
- strong sense of right and wrong—badgers child when perceived as wrong

AS A CHILD

- some expend high energy manipulating parents to get own way
- often defiant
- resists control—feel they know more than parents
- can be critical of parents
- fights constantly with siblings for control and power
- subconsciously hides insecurities and emotional needs
- can remain aloof and distant from camaraderie of family
- not creative in play—requires others to entertain him or her
- unhappy complainers—parents can never do enough right
- finds sincere compliments difficult to give
- some are dramatic and overreactive to pain
- some want to be catered to when sick

AS A FRIEND

- insensitive and unemotional
- doesn't like to admit the need for friendships
- remains detached from sharing self completely
- enters friendships asking, "What's in it for me?"
- listens only when convenient
- maintains mostly rational friendships
- tries to control group activities
- expects friends to do things their way

- impatient with others behavior, thinking and tardiness
- negative, critical and judgmental of others
- feels it is more important to be right than agreeable
- blunt or rude when angered
- boring (susceptible to ruts i.e., television)
- expects to be entertained while waiting for action to begin
- stubborn
- denies any personal inadequacies or responsibility

AS A COMMITTED COMPANION

- primarily concerned with self-gratification
- prioritizes work over personal relationships
- demanding and arrogant
- dominates relationships with verbal skills
- hides insecurities
- critical of companion for imperfections
- lacks sensitivity
- often unaware of intimacy and rejects its priority in a relationship

How To Develop a Positive Connection with Reds

Do:

1. Present issues logically
2. Demand their attention and respect
3. Be direct, brief and specific in conversation
4. Be productive and efficient
5. Offer them leadership opportunities
6. Verbalize your feelings
7. Support their decisive nature
8. Promote their intelligent reasoning where appropriate
9. Be prepared with facts and figures
10. Respect their need to make their own decisions their own way

Don't:

1. Embarass them in front of others
2. Argue from an emotional perspective
3. Always use authoritarian approach
4. Use physical punishment
5. Be slow and indecisive
6. Expect a personal and intimate relationship
7. Attack them personally
8. Take their arguments personally
9. Wait for them to solicit your opinion
10. Demand constant social interaction (allow for alone time)

CHAPTER FIVE

Blues: The Do-Goolers

Blues: The Do-Gooders

Emotional and Admired

The Blues are often the most admired of all the personalities. They represent so many of the virtues we aspire to, such as honesty, empathy, self-sacrifice, loyalty, sincerity and self-discipline. They seem to come by these virtues naturally which creates an image of righteousness and respect. They resemble a lighted beacon of goodness and truth—a standard of excellence for the rest of us to appreciate and aspire to. Blues appreciate creativity, committed relationships, and disciplined achievement. With these combined assets, a strong and purposeful individual inevitably evolves. They are deeply committed, fiercely loyal to people and well-behaved members of society. They are highly opinionated and tough competitors for any personality to face because they generally base all opinions on emotion and moral principle. Although Blues can be logical, they are more likely to respond to an emotional plea.

For Blues, life is emotionally a double-edge sword. On the positive side they are giving and sensitive. On the negative end they can be unforgiving and too sensitive. In fact, they can be so sensitive that they stop giving at all. A common statement by my Blue patients is "My emotions have ruled me all my life." Perhaps their true Achilles heel (Achilles was a legendary warrior in greek mythology whose only vulnerability was in his heel) is their unbridled emotions. They want so badly to feel loved. They seek understanding from others while often refusing to understand themselves. Blues ride a powerful rollercoaster of emotions. Sensitive to all kinds of trivial matters, they constantly find themselves vulnerable to emotional trauma.

Depression is frequently experienced by Blues. Allowing their hearts to rule their minds, they often think and behave irrationally. The following example comes from the journal notes of a Blue patient. It is an extreme case of the "moody Blues." However, it clearly expresses the frustration most Blues experience with accepting other's behavior when it doesn't meet their high standards and often unrealistic expectations. One evening she was reflecting on her recently dissolved marriage and wrote the following letter in her journal.

"Happy Anniversary to me. I hate Jason (her husband). I hate myself. I hate everyone, especially I hate living. I am so angry and bitter it feels like I cannot go on living because it is too uncomfortable. There is no joy—no hope. I feel only bitterness and hatred and anger at life, even at God because things are so awful. I don't even like people who want to help me or support me. I wish I could just go away from everyone and everything. Nothing would be better, of course.

There is just no way around this portion of life that I can see. Perhaps if I would humble myself and pray for some relief I might get it, but I'm too mad for that even. I'm mad at God! I'm mad at Jesus! I'm mad at my parents! I'm mad at my kids! I'm mad at myself! And I *hate* Jason! I would like to see harm come to him I think. But then I'd be mad because he doesn't even have life insurance. They'd probably want me to pay for his funeral too.

I just hate everything. I wish I would die, but I can't and that makes me mad too. I'm mad that life is so rotten and there's no way out. So I'll just be mad for a while longer because I don't see any viable options. But I want to be clear about communicating this: LIFE SUCKS AND I HATE ALL OF IT!!!!!

I'm so tired of being "RESPONSIBLE" for everything—even the kids. I wish someone would put me in a mental institution so I wouldn't have to deal with anything. Or maybe I could have an accident and be in the hospital so I could be taken care of and have no responsibility. Then I wouldn't have to take care of my kids or anyone—or worry about Jason's bills. I hate him! I hate everything! Life seems so unfair. I don't want any of this. I don't want to grow or progress or get stronger.

I want to be left alone for a while by everyone—God included! I don't want anyone to expect anything from me because I'm tired of being capable. I'm tired of people saying how great I'm doing. I'm tired of the whole bullcrap situation. In fact, I'm even tired of writing this depressing garbage so goodbye."

When my patient shared this with me, she no longer felt the anger displayed in her journal notes. Instead, she felt rather foolish, at times laughing while she shared her writings with me. Three days later she called me and said, "I can't believe this. I feel exactly the way I felt when I wrote those notes. What's wrong with me?! I feel like I'm losing my mind!" Actually, she had never found her mind (logical thinking). She was victimized by an undisciplined heart.

Blues see the world through positive and healthy emotional eyes as well. They care deeply for those elements of living which tug at their heart. Weddings, parades and birthdays give great cause for celebration, but Blues even see beyond the events and take time to reflect on the lives of those involved. They think of their own weddings (past, present or future) and what it means to be in love. They consider all the hours it takes to prepare the costumes and mechanics of a parade as it passes by. Blues wonder how the aging grandmother feels on her 70th birthday, and feel mesmerized by a three year old blowing candles out on a cake. They "make" time for sharing the important moments of life.

Committed and Loyal

Their life is a sequence of commitments. Committing to relationships is perhaps their greatest strength. They enjoy companionship and willingly sacrifice personal gain in order to share intimate relationships. Blues give freely of themselves in valued relationships.

Their willingness to commit to relationships affords Blues deep friendships which often last a lifetime. They are highly dependable and consider a verbal promise as binding as any written contract. They pride themselves in maintaining long term relationships. This admirable trait of loyalty gives credibility to the concept that Blues usually enjoy far richer quality in their relationships than any other personality type.

Blues are completely loyal to people. Blues remain committed through the good and the bad times. When one realizes the depth of their commitment it is easy to understand why fair or foul weather has little impact on a Blue's loyalty. An excellent example of this commitment is exemplified in the life of one of my Blue patients, Jenny. She had never enjoyed her mother while growing up. In fact, she struggled simply to maintain a civil relationship despite her mother's constant attempts to sabotage her. Her mother repeatedly humiliated her by calling her names and mocking her for her lack of popularity with boys through the dating years. Despite the obvious favoritism mom had displayed for Jenny's older brothers and sisters, Jenny was the only one of the children willing to undertake the tremendous responsibility of caring for her invalid mother during the final painful days of her life.

Our paths crossed when Jenny sought psychological help in order to sustain the necessary courage to face this woman she had so often struggled with through the years. Jenny stayed close to her mother's bedside despite her mother's repeated abuses and lack of appreciation until she died. Would other personalities have innately loved as much?

Perfectionist

Blues are usually perfectionists. Blues are highly critical of themselves and others. They have such unrealistic expectations that they can never satisfy themselves nor expect others to meet their level of excellence. This is one reason they are difficult employers and parents. I call my Blue daughter, "little miss hard-to-please." They really do want things done right. Unfortunately, right is defined as whatever and however *they* want things done.

Blues are typically skeptical about their own creative talents. They are such perfectionists that they often hide their skills and abilities because they fear they aren't good enough. It's most unfortunate because Blues are so talented and perhaps the most creative of all the colors. However, Blues are highly insecure and often fear the possibility of rejection in displaying themselves publicly with their enviable creativity and talents.

High Expectations and Demanding

Blues often struggle with effective verbal communication and subsequently others often have no idea what Blue's real expectations are, nor how to proceed in meeting them. Even knowing their expectations is not always helpful because meeting their unrealistic expectations would take more energy than others are willing to give. I'm referring specifically to a parent's expectation of straight A's on a report card, spotless rooms, chores done promptly and properly everyday. I wonder if Blues don't represent eighty percent of the parents who scream at their children. We would all scream if we had their perfectionistic expectations. They confuse their priorities and neglect to realize that a more simplistic, rational approach to expectations would be healthier and far more productive.

Blue employers demand that their employees swear an allegiance of time and talent to the company. A report worth doing at all is worth doing well. They expect excellence on projects that probably shouldn't require all the attention to detail the employer expects. They don't say what they want but magically believe that everyone thinks like they do and will produce results like they do. Blues don't often delegate well. They stand over others like a "mother hen" in order to protect them from error. This protection is construed by Blues to mean nurturing. It is actually distrust. They believe that by maintaining a strong emotional tie with each employee that they are being supportive and promoting effective employee relations. Then, they ask, why do so many feel like they are being strangled or spied on? It's so difficult to convince Blues that their intentions are not clear and their expectations are so demanding that subordinates often wish they would go back to their own office and leave everyone else alone. However, employees don't often tell their Blue boss this because the boss is overly sensitive and usually means well, so no one wants to hurt his or her feelings. Instead of honest, direct communication, Blues typically get dishonest patronizing from employees.

Self-Disciplined and Stable

Blues must have written the slogan, *"If a job's worth doing, it's worth doing well."* Self-discipline comes from deep within the Blue's personality core. Throwing themselves into a project often brings out the best in Blues. They seek opportunities to develop their many talents. This perpetual exercising of self-discipline brings stability and order to their lives. Many people learn to depend on Blues because of their steady and predictable nature. They provide us with a sense of endearing security. They thrive in environments where security is valued and nourished. With proper support and cooperation they will bring creative gifts of the highest possible caliber. Their gifts always come from the heart.

Self-Sacrificing and Nurturing

With rare exceptions, Blues think of others before themselves and bring love to the lives of those they touch. They love to serve. Doing for others gives them tremendous satisfaction. Being productive is important, but producing for people they care about seems to make the contribution mean much more to them. *They always seek purpose in their life.* They want the sense of having lived for something more than simply earning a wage or changing a diaper.

Unforgiving and Resentful

Ironically, Blues *give* more than any personality but *forgive* the least. I have encountered many Blues who have yet to forgive their parents for damages done during childhood. It is quite easy to find Blues in an audience. I simply ask for a show of hands from those who can remember all the bad things their kindergarten teacher did to them. Blues always remember. Reds don't remember. They already took care of the teacher with tacks on her chair or reported her for child abuse to the principal. Yellows thought it was funny and enjoyed the attention whether it was good or bad. And Whites aren't sure they were in kindergarten so what's to remember?!

One of Blue's most self-destructive weaknesses is resentment. It often goes hand in hand with their excellent memory. One sixty-seven year old patient resented her White husband for numerous reasons covering a span of fifty years of married life. She was so angry at him once that she secretly took her wedding dress down from her closet and donated it to a charitable organization. Needless to say, her motives were less than charitable. She kept his limited self-esteem in negative check by constantly undermining him. She exemplifies the Blue's need to get even and their struggle with letting go of resentment.

Worry and Guilt

Blues also seem to worry about everything. All this excess worry makes it only possible to handle so much excitement in one day. I remember one patient who had a major decision to make. Her decision was between leaving for the East coast on June 11th for two weeks to visit family, or going to an all expenses paid three-day church convention with her husband which ended June 7th. That only left her three days to repack and get ready for her trip back East. But she always enjoyed being with her husband at the church conventions. She didn't know whether to stay home and be ready for her trip to the East or go to the convention. She was also afraid that her kids would tear the house apart while she was gone. (We're talking about 25 year old twins.) Blues do not appreciate being rushed through life regardless of the quality of events they are being rushed to enjoy. Worrying about others, rather than productively engaging in activities of their own, can be a serious problem for Blues.

A thirty year old woman experienced worry whenever she drove on the freeway. When driving in the middle lane, if a car changed lanes behind her, she immediately cross-examined herself by asking, "Am I driving too fast? Too slow? Are my brake lights disturbing other drivers?"

Worry and guilt generally mark the path to most Blues' homes. They can be "guilted" into almost anything. They often neglect to see that their true motives in many circumstances are based on guilt. For wrongs they think they've done, Blues will seemingly chastise themselves forever.

Appropriate and Sincere

Blues value culture and appropriate behavior. They understand the value of manners and propriety in society. Blues deem it their personal responsibility to serve as the moral "watch dogs" for society. They seek always to preserve the dignity and quality of human life.

They are comfortably obedient to laws and authority. Blues think society requires structure and discipline in order to function properly. No other strength labels the Blues as uniquely as does the trait of sincerity. One of life's great treasures is to attain and experience their trust. Life cannot bestow on anyone a more deserving or gratifying reward than the sincere appreciation and trust of a Blue friend, employer or family member.

Purposeful and Dedicated

They have a strong work ethic and often find their lives cluttered with "necessary responsibilities" with little or no time for spontaneous playtime. Play is often seen as frivolous and unproductive. It's not uncommon to see a Blue mother productively knitting or reading at a park while her children climb, swing, run and devour their free time with no concern for anything but momentary pleasure. Blues envy the peace of mind and carefree attitude Yellows glide through life with. They often cry "unfair" and wish either the other personalities would enjoy life less, or at least reward the Blues for their dedication to the more noble concept of purposeful work. Unfortunately, neither wish is likely to come true.

Moody and Complex

Another tell-tale sign of Blues is their mood swings. They never wake up happy or sad. They have to think about it first. If they are happy or sad during the day, it is because they choose to be. They can't seem to simply accept an emotion without taking full responsibility for selecting it.

Blues are highly complex individuals. They are not easy to understand. They have such powerful strengths and debilitating limitations. They are sensitive, tense, caring, critical, giving and unforgiving at the same time. They are comprised of many extremes. Their focus is on emotional rather than rational connections. Despite their emotional focus, they are often guilty of emotional rigidity. In other words, they get stuck in emotional ruts. They lose perspective and find themselves misunderstood. Unable to express their feelings effectively, the Blues struggle to pump more energy into frustrating relationships to experience the intimacy which is essential for them in order to feel their life has purpose. Sometimes the energy they pump is healthy and sometimes it is destructive. The complexity of the Blue personality frustrates Blues as much as other personalities who have to interact with them. Perhaps this explains why Blues are so critical of themselves as well as others.

Self-Righteous and Insecure

Each personality color shares insecurity as a common denominator. However, no personality shares it as publicly as Blues. Blues have a powerful personality. They feel driven to participate in life. They voice their opinions, albeit sometimes only within the safe walls of their homes. They have strong values and belief systems. However, they are torn by guilt feelings, resulting from unrealistic expectations caused by a perfectionistic attitude and skepticism. They are often caught between wanting to be involved and fearing their ability to be successful with their involvement.

The complexity of this insecurity is further enhanced by their unique self-righteous attitude. Perhaps no statement describes this attitude better than the bumper sticker, "Those of us who think they know everything (referring to the Reds) annoy those of us who really do." Unlike the vocal, arrogant Reds, Blues silently remind themselves how unfortunate it is that others must remain so ignorant. There is a certain smugness connected with Blues. They piously view the world with a suspicious eye. They have limited hope that others will ever fully understand life as they do. This judicious piety taints Blues with a pessimistic nature. They wish others would care enough to adopt the Blue's attitude of perfection. They are frustrated with the realization that many people prefer to accept life rather than modify it. Self-righteousness does not breed intimacy. Rather it promotes emotional distance and deception.

Blue Limitations

Blues probably experience their greatest enemy in themselves. Their self-righteous attitudes are merely a guise for deep insecurity. They are often too emotional and judgmental to enjoy intimacy. They continually depress themselves and others with unrealistic expectations of perfection. Lacking trust, they find themselves skeptical and suspicious of others. Blues often find themselves bitter, resentful and unforgiving of those who have crossed them in life. Overwhelming guilt and worry continue to drive them inward, seeking solace from the only one who truly understands them—themselves. Blues are hard to please and tense about schedules. They are moody and find leadership a difficult dilemma. Blues aren't generally playful or spontaneous. In anger, they are the personality most likely to feel like, "Life's a bitch and then you die." They often fail to see the humor in life. Blues become angry when others find them to be irrational and emotionally rigid in relationships. Blues exemplify the well-known phrase, "We have found the enemy. The enemy is us."

Blue Strengths

Like the earth which sustained and nurtured our earliest ancestors, Blues are also steady, ordered and enduring. They grant us culture, beauty and emotional sincerity. Blues love with a passion. They see the finer things in life as intimate relationships and creative accomplishments rather than material possessions. They bring culture and decency to home and society. They appreciate uplifting experiences and feel most comfortable in creative and productive environments. They want a sense of purpose in their life and willingly sacrifice personal luxuries in order to attain more meaningful accomplishments.

They are highly committed individuals. Loyalty to people and sincerity in relationships (at home and work) are their trademarks. They believe in all causes that bring a higher quality to the human experience. They listen with endearing empathy and speak with emotional zeal. Blues truly value their connectedness to people and enjoy the accomplishments of others. With perfection as their guide, they stretch for the best they can find from within themselves. They expect the same in their fellow beings. Obediently, they accept the need for authority and put their energy into supporting law and order. They are essentially the glue that binds society together. Blues give us cause to prioritize our lives, giving preference to personal relationships and quality achievements. They add that special touch of excellence as they freely commit their hearts and souls to the betterment of us all in our shared journey through life.

Blues Strengths

AS AN INDIVIDUAL

- sees life as a serious endeavor
- appreciates beauty and detail
- has a strong aesthetic sense
- stable and dependable (plow horse versus race horse)
- sincere and emotionally deep
- analytically oriented (concerned with why one behaves as he/she does)
- high achiever
- deep sense of purpose

AS A COMMUNICATOR

- able to enjoy sensitive and deep conversation
- strong skills in empathizing with others
- remembers feelings and thoughts shared in conversation
- willing to give conversations time to run their course
- prefers small groups

AS A GOAL SETTER

- highly disciplined
- receptive to other's suggestions
- strong goal orientation
- plans well and superb follow through

AS A CAREER PERSON

- excellent behind-the-scenes worker

- respectful of employer because of employer's position
- enjoys detail and schedules
- receptive to creative thinking
- gives more of self than required or expected

AS A PARENT

- encourages academics and/or trade development in children
- excellent trainer of skills (i.e., manners, study habits)
- very observant
- empathic and sensitive
- sincere and loyal to children
- keeps home clean and cozy
- seeks to understand children's behavior
- self-sacrificing
- excellent in long term commitments

AS A CHILD

- proper and behaved
- easily disciplined verbally
- concerned about being a good family member
- sensitive and concerned about other family members
- loyal to parents and siblings regardless of relationship
- seeks learning opportunities

AS A FRIEND

- loyal forever once friendship is established
- genuine concern for other person's well-being
- remembers special holidays and promotes celebrations
- encouraging in times of trouble
- willing to commit time to the relationship

AS A COMMITTED COMPANION

- prioritizes the relationship over other activities
- considers spouse first in decision-making
- responsible for making ongoing contribution to relationship

- enjoys sharing intimate feelings with companion
- values intimacy and places high priority on it

CAREERS MOST LIKELY TO ATTRACT BLUES

Teacher	Banker	Nurse
Homemaker	Clergy/Minister	Engineer
Psychotherapist	Accountant	Librarian
Computer Programmer	Politician	Journalist
Musician	Architect	Carpenter

Note: Blues are most capable of adapting in the career world.

PERSONALITIES WHO APPEAR TO BE POSITIVE BLUES

Abraham Lincoln	Barbara Bush	Walt Disney

BLUE NATIONS

United States	England	Denmark

Blues Limitations

AS AN INDIVIDUAL

- highly emotional
- smug and self-righteous
- controlling and/or envious of other's success when too easily obtained
- strong perfection and performance orientation
- self-abusive (verbally)

AS A COMMUNICATOR

- tends to lecture and overkill issues
- feels intense on many issues
- rigid with principles and unwilling to negotiate
- fears risking self in conversation
- argues primarily from emotional perspective
- strong expectation for others to be sensitive and deep
- expects others to read his or her mind and know his or her feelings

AS A GOAL SETTER

- sets unrealistic goals

- easily discouraged when unsuccessful in accomplishments
- easily frustrated with lack of team cooperation
- expects others to understand his or her goals and make them a priority

AS A CAREER PERSON

- feels others are not capable of doing things as well as he or she
- craves security in career
- feels inadequate with natural talents and creativity
- shys away from public exposure and performance
- establishes high and often unrealistic expectations for self and others
- tend to over-plan and over-prepare
- critical of self and other's work
- over-extends self

AS A PARENT

- blames children for being unappreciative of parenting efforts
- can be moody and unpredictable
- easily irritated by other's mistakes and shortcomings
- usually loves others with strings attached
- tends to give heavy doses of guilt to children
- lacks ability to relax
- requires a purpose in order to play
- controlling of children's lifestyle and overprotective
- too precise and exact with expectations
- feels a clean home is a high priority
- accepts guilt feelings too easily and readily
- not spontaneous with activities
- frustrates children with unrealistic expectations
- strong sense of right and wrong—badgers child when perceived as wrong
- lectures children

AS A CHILD

- easily frustrated
- feels guilty over minor concerns
- moody and emotional (cries instead of facing issues)

- feelings are easily hurt
- martyr-like and complains about life
- self-esteem is dependent on outside influences
- has difficulty relaxing and often feels uncomfortable
- withholds affection if angered
- waits for parent to initiate ideas and then criticizes unacceptable suggestions

AS A FRIEND

- highly insecure about other's acceptance and approval
- feels rejected easily
- when depressed or depressive—feels it is friend's job to understand
- can be revengeful and bitter if crossed or scarred emotionally
- critical of friend's principles or activities if not similar
- expects friends to maintain strong loyalty
- wishes friends would communicate more often
- rarely playful and spontaneous

AS A COMMITTED COMPANION

- blames others for his or her unhappiness ("if only you were more...")
- demands affection and intimacy
- demands time and attention of partner
- highly manipulative in seeking support or understanding
- suspicious of other's motives (distrustful)
- unforgiving of past misunderstandings and wrong doings
- clings to companion too much
- withholds feelings when frightened he or she may be rejected

How to Develop a Positive Connection with Blues

Do:

1. Emphasize their security in the relationship
2. Be sensitive and soft spoken in your approach
3. Be sincere and genuine
4. Behave appropriately and well-mannered
5. Limit their risk level

6. Promote their creativity
7. Appreciate them
8. Allow ample time for them to gather their thoughts before expressing themselves
9. Be loyal
10. Do thorough analysis before making presentations

Don't:

1. Make them feel guilty
2. Be rude or abrupt
3. Promote too much change
4. Expect spontaneity
5. Abandon them
6. Expect them to bounce back easily or quickly from depression
7. Demand perfection (they already expect too much from themselves)
8. Push them too quickly into making decisions
9. Expect them to forgive quickly when crossed
10. Demand immediate action

CHAPTER SIX

Whites: The Peace Keepers

Peaceful and Diplomatic

Whites represent most completely the peacemaker. They sincerely believe in the value of diplomacy and seek diligently to promote cooperation at all cost.

How many times have we all said, "Will everybody just settle down? All I want right now is some PEACE!" At that moment, if we could simply transform everyone into a White personality our wish for peace would become reality. Every parent prays for a child with a White personality. Every teacher deserves at least one student with a White personality. Everybody is benefitted by intimately knowing one. Whites offer us all a model for gentle human dignity. They quietly move through life with an easy, unruffled style. Whites appreciate the cooperative nature of mankind and repeatedly promote their preference for a peaceful coexistence among all living things.

Whites are usually difficult to know. They operate on a self-serving, power orientation, yet so subtly that it often leaves one wondering whether they are the manipulated or the manipulator. Whites are often lost, inviting others to rescue and protect them in life. Caught in their own neediness, Whites are often handicapped in asserting themselves and growing. Rather, they remain victims, often silently traumatized by their anger, rather than honestly acknowledging their feelings. Whites can be very timid and shy, which limits them from living life to the fullest. They may depend on others to make their life happen.

Insecure and Non-Assertive

Whites can be difficult to read. Whites appear to approach life so simply that one may misinterpret them to be at peace when their real feelings may actually be fear, timidity, laziness or personal inadequacy. They are such good-natured individuals that people generally prefer not to ruffle White's feathers or make waves. People typically ignore White's limitations and acknowledge White's strengths. This is particularly difficult for those who are intimately involved with Whites (i.e., parents, spouses, children, teachers, friends). Ignoring White's deficiencies protects and limits them from facing themselves. Other personalities actually cripple Whites and make their personal development more difficult. Protecting Whites and ignoring their limitations ultimately forces healthy Whites to stand up and be confrontive, which is directly contrary to their innate nature.

A terribly regrettable incident which illuminates the White self-doubt and unwillingness to confront others comes from a female patient, twenty years of age. She experienced sexual intercourse for the first time at sixteen in the back seat of a car. She and her drunk date fooled around while his friend drove the car through town. Immediately following intercourse, he threw up from drinking too much alcohol. He was suddenly furious. She was concerned about the mess in his car and his angry feelings so she comforted him by saying, "That's okay. I'll help clean it up." Without the slightest concern for her feelings, he remarked, "I'm not worried about that. I'm worried about my girlfriend finding out I've been drinking again." Had they not just experienced an "intimate" sexual encounter? Wasn't she special to him? She continued this absurdity without confrontation by staying involved with this guy for another year before she could finally let go.

Whites can be very clingy. They can follow you through life, never assuming any independence or leadership of their own. They often make others the core of their existence and neglect to develop their own sense of purpose and direction. Some Whites become so attached to one individual, that they refuse to develop outside interests or make any commitments which would separate them from their relationship. A couple in their thirties were dating seriously when the woman (Red) decided to take a weekend cruise with a girlfriend. Her boyfriend (White) was terribly hurt and insecure. She was finally tired of his whining and told him she was going with her girlfriend and could never consider marrying him if he didn't get his own life together without always waiting for her to include him in her plans. She was thrilled when he announced that he was going to visit a good friend in Montana the same weekend she went on the cruise. However, after careful consideration of what motivated his behavior it became apparent that he was simply satisfying her request for independence in order not to jeopardize their potential marriage plans. Subsequently, she further promoted the idea that he be the one to initiate his independent plans next time rather than simply reacting to hers.

Doubtful and Dependent

Whites doubt themselves so much that they constantly demand proof of acceptance. "Prove to me," they say, "that you accept me. Stay with me always and be there for me, for I am inadequate and you are strong." The price is high when one tries to rescue, accept and protect a clingy White. It is much like holding a man by his wrists when he is falling from a cliff. The longer you hold on, the heavier he becomes. Yet, he feels safer in your grasp than to trust himself and assist in the rescue by climbing back up. The nobility of the rescue soon loses its shine and you become the victim. If you "care", you feel obligated to hold on for life, giving up a life of your own in order to save his. If you let go, society rebukes you for giving up and selfishly seeking your own rewards elsewhere. Such a dilemma is commonly experienced by clinging Whites and those they encounter in life.

In order to encourage this unhealthy, albeit, seemingly secure type of relationship, Whites seek to please others. Whites often get other's support through service. This service to others typically comes with strings attached. Usually the strings come in the form of protection, security, control, support, and direction.

Jeff had been the perfect child (Whites usually are) and resisted "rocking the boat" for any reason with his retired parents. Knowing this, Jeff's parents repeatedly did things that controlled his choices despite the fact that he had been married once, held a very responsible job and maintained a desirable lifestyle. Now he wanted very much to marry an Oriental woman. Jeff is Caucasian. His mother flatly refused to entertain the idea and the father supported his "traumatized" wife. The man felt abandoned. Jeff had been a wonderful, caring son. When his only brother had turned his back on their parents for their meddling, Jeff remained loyal to his parents. Now he felt torn in half. He was devoted and loyal to his parents as well as his girlfriend. Notice that I didn't mention loyalty to himself. He had not yet developed loyalty to himself. He didn't count, yet. He experienced his value and self-worth through others. Now he needed to find himself and challenge his secure relationship with his parents if he was ever to know self-respect. Through months of therapy and inner struggling, he freed himself of his parents and pursued a life representative of his values and beliefs. Jeff eventually married his Oriental fiance. Jeff will never feel as welcomed or "loved" by his parents as before, but he now recognizes that pleasing himself appropriately is far more gratifying than living his life to please others.

Tolerant and Patient

Unless other personalities push Whites into a combative stance, they can tolerate an enormous amount of pain. Whites are tolerant of other's disagreeable behavior regardless of the personal discomfort they may feel. One mother (White) watched her young teenage son leave home on two separate occasions "just because he felt like it." He simply wanted to live somewhere else. This mother was deeply concerned and maintained positive communication despite her son's inappropriate and selfish behavior.

I recently asked one hundred students at the university to identify the trait they felt was most important for a successful parent to develop. Independently of each other, ninety-five percent of them ranked *patience* as the most significant virtue for successful parenting. I was amazed at this overwhelming response from these young adults. What about love, discipline, and leadership? Why hadn't they given the edge to communication (the buzz word of the eighties) or some other well-known attribute? The students offered me a valuable insight into parenting and the White personality. They said, "patience indicates a trust in the human dignity—a belief that people can make the right choices in life when given the free agency to act for themselves." What a powerful statement! I have appreciated the White personality with new depth since that educational experience.

Impressionable

Whites are quite impressionable. They observe everything. Like an owl, they keep a watchful eye on the human condition. This can be very traumatic for Whites who experience a negative childhood. One patient tearfully remembered outloud her last encounter with her father. He had a fight with her mom and was leaving their yard. She was five years old and asked if she could go with him. She knew they were fighting but never considered he was leaving for good. She thought he was going to the store and she wanted to be with him. He said she couldn't come and he left. She went inside and saw her mom sobbing and realized this was more serious than any other time. She never developed trust or the capacity for sharing her feelings freely with **anyone** after this devastating experience. She still calls him for special occasions but nothing has erased the pain she experienced that day as a five year old watching her daddy leave and later realizing he'd never come home again.

Withhold Feelings

Whites don't trust freely. Whites usually hold their true feelings very close to the heart, safely tucked away from others who may not approve of or value their feelings. One intellectually brilliant man offered to tutor his Harvard roommates in medical school free of charge. He later realized that it was his way of expressing his warm feelings to them without having to acknowledge it. It provided a safe method for supposed intimacy. He regrets now that he never shared himself. He shared his knowledge because he was secure in that. Looking back, he realizes that he may have been able to establish good friendships if he had been able to trust others with his inner feelings and thoughts.

Blendable and Kind

The gentle nature of Whites typically shines through regardless of their level of trust. They remain kind and agreeable with almost everyone they meet. Whites are so blendable. A sure sign of a White personality is the individual who genuinely feels like a rainbow of colors. Whites can find themselves in all personalities because they are so capable of blending in with each personality.

Unproductive Dreamers

Whites often remain unproductive dreamers. They have tremendous plans and can often fancy themselves to be somewhere other than where they currently are, but dreams remain just that—dreams, until one can focus and produce. These flaws leave Whites and those intimately connected with Whites, unsettled and disappointed. Whites are the least effective, of all the personalities at implementing changes. (Yellows run a close second.)

I remember one White accountant who could never decide what he really wanted to do professionally. Several firms he worked for had folded and each time he had remained until the end rather than seeking other employment with the realization that his current job would be terminated. His wife was terribly distressed with his ambivalence and yet remained highly supportive. Finally he shared how his real dream in life was to own a small food franchise. He had the necessary business skills and his wife had terrific people skills. Years passed and nothing ever came of this man's dream. His wife remained supportive and successfully pursued her own career. However, he was never able to commit to his dream of owning his own business.

Unmotivated

This lack of direction breeds a lack of motivation. Whites are highly unmotivated until they establish goals and commit to accomplishing those goals. Unfortunately, this is much easier to discuss than to do. One White friend of mine would experience moments of brilliance when he would "see the light" and commit to a particular goal. Within a short time span, as with a shooting star, this brilliance and excitement would be explained away and lost, until another momentary flash of encouragement arrived. Like many Whites, setting and accomplishing his goals didn't come easily. However, goals are the only hope for unmotivated Whites. Until they are able to establish direction in their lives, Whites often remain unsettled and discouraged.

Accepting

Whites are conceivably capable of being the best friends to all personalities. They find accepting others a rather simple task. They have such tolerant expectations of others, that people value their companionship and seek their non-judgmental relationships. Whites enjoy doing almost anything with anyone, anywhere. They can enjoy a vast variety of people and experiences and subsequently often find themselves in unusual relationships or life situations.

Boring and Lazy

Whites miss many potentially wonderful moments in life because they look to others rather than themselves for excitement and relevance in life. Perhaps the word that Whites like least to accept responsibility for is "boring." Yet, Whites can be just that—boring. They depend on others to make life happen. Perhaps the example which best depicts this dependency is this typical directionless relationship between two Whites.

Two Whites dated for years before deciding to marry. Their courtship consisted primarily of shared television and quiet moments together. They married and after five years they decided they were wrong for each other. Neither was happy or finding life particularly fulfilling. Through the next five years this couple remained married, but separate in their dreams and aspirations. He pursued a college degree and she moved to another city to become a police officer. Neither committed to share decision making. Neither made the decision to leave. After seven more wasted years of living apart but not choosing truly separate lives, they divorced. Why so long? Both admitted they couldn't agree on who should file the papers!

Whites are vulnerable to wasting time in life. They may give it away to boredom, laziness or dull reluctance to change. I have seen wives leave husbands, husbands leave wives, employees leave employers, kids and parents leave each other, friendships dissolve and a myriad of other potentially wonderful relationships end due primarily to boredom. The worst part is that the person leaving often feels very guilty because the grounds for separation aren't as dramatic as infidelity, distrust, or abuse. Life with a boring White can be a devastating and draining existence.

Lazy, (just try and get one moving in the early morning) and reluctant, the White personality often moves sluggishly through life. They are in no hurry to experience life. They feel certain life will wait for them. They use the Chinese saying, "Everything comes to he who waits" as a motto. Everything does come (good and bad) to he who waits. However, whatever he gets when it finally comes may be a far cry from what he would have chosen given the chance to actively select a lifestyle.

Timid and Emotionally Unsure

Whites remind me of the cowardly lion seeking courage in the movie "The Wizard of Oz." They can be a frightened group of individuals. This should not imply that they are necessarily afraid of physical danger but rather emotional trauma. One young woman feared rejection so much that she developed seizures. She was taunted by kids in elementary school and when she could no longer handle it, she developed a method for diverting the attention from her emotional insecurities to a physical handicap (seizures). This eventually resulted in adult coddling and peer avoidance. Unfortunately, adult adulation wasn't her need, and peer avoidance provided little comfort when other kids ran off to slumber parties and ate lunch together at school.

Gentle and Even-Tempered

The White child is truly a gift from heaven. They are so simple. They do not come with great fanfare. They are usually the easiest babies to care for. There is a unique gentleness to these children that promotes family harmony. They are the children who travel through life with an even-temper. New experiences can traumatize a White child. However, they typically enjoy a peaceful, casual existence.

Aimless and Misguided

Sometimes Whites approach life too casually. This can be seen in their aimless and misguided nature. Particularly frustrating aspects of the Whites aimless and misguided nature, is the energy that the rest of us must expend to make up for them: White children forgetting lunches; White friends neglecting to pick up the children for baseball practice; White husbands unable to select a career direction; and White siblings not willing to develop their own friendships put a strain on the other personalities who have to always include them in their plans. Whites rarely realize how selfish their limitations are. By presenting themselves as kind but helpless souls, they often seem to ignore the pressure their inadequacy places on everyone else.

How enjoyable can life be when you have to constantly remind someone to brush their teeth, call the hotel for reservations, remind what time school or work begins, etc., etc., etc. Whites often respond to these reminders with a casual (albeit disdaining) remark like, "Why do you have to get so huffy about everything? Who's life is it anyway? Go on and mind your own business and leave me alone." The frustration mounts for the other personalities who have much greater expectations for Whites than Whites have for themselves. Whites are notorious for requiring assistance in planning and processing life. They are less notorious for accepting, and yet equally capable of resisting, the very assistance they require.

Indecisive

Whites rarely seek leadership positions. They are more comfortable in a follower or less involved role, leaving group decision making to others. They are uncomfortable making decisions which may be wrong and avoid responsibilities that require it. Whites would rather just accept other's decisions than assert themselves with opinions. One patient asked his wife, "Honey, on this test of Dr. Hartman's, it wants to know if I'm decisive. Do you think I am or not?" We all shared a good laugh, recognizing that he never realized what he was asking until she said, "Honey, somehow I think you just answered your own question better than I could ever hope to!"

Silent and Stubborn

Whites can be very strong and stubborn. One of my White patients hated high school. He despised homework and all the demands of education. He was particularly bright but unwilling to engage in conflict with either parents or teachers. How does one satisfy everyone (including themselves) when there is no agreement on what must be done? This was his dilemma. He hated homework and they demanded that it be done. For one solid semester in eighth grade, this young man, Michael, did every homework assignment and never turned one of them in to his teachers. Every night his parents would ask him if he did his homework and he would answer "yes." When grades slipped dramatically and they requested to see his work, he promptly showed them. By the end of the semester, his parents thought they were going crazy. Were his teachers out to get their son? They had seen his work but the teachers refused to accept that he had completed it. This case depicts the silent, strong, stubborn nature of Whites.

Whites prefer the strong silent treatment because they are uncomfortable with confrontation. It is very difficult to live with people who silently resent your behavior. Whites take advantage of other's curiosity by refusing to share their feelings openly. Other personalities struggle to understand Whites. Whites often feel very deeply but struggle to express their feelings to others. One White father took an intolerable amount of abuse from his Red step-son for years in order to maintain peace in the home. His wife refused to allow him to discipline the child. He simply suffered in silence. Finally, after multiple problems including molestation, school failures, etc., the natural mother allowed the father to take a more active role in disciplining his step-son. He had never released his true anger for all the disruptions this child had brought to his life. With his wife's approval, he gladly went on the offensive. It was almost as if he relished this new found freedom as he physically struck his son whenever he could find justification.

White Limitations

Whites often seem boring and uninvolved. They are often unwilling to set goals. They frequently refuse to pay the price of involvement because they may fear the inevitable aspects of confrontation or rejection. This fear keeps them from experiencing intimacy. Their indecision limits their accomplishments. In order to feel secure, Whites pay great attention to the needs of others and strive at all costs to please those they encounter in life. They reluctantly express themselves, preferring to let others believe as they will. Meanwhile, the Whites go about their lives as they choose, avoiding conflict and confrontations. Whites silently accept whatever comes their way. What they don't value, they stubbornly discard in time. They often do not bring to their lives those desirable experiences which require the effort of risk, leadership and honest expression.

White Strengths

On the positive side, Whites are the satisfied ones. They are contented and agreeable individuals who easily accomodate others through life. They complement every personality regardless of their differences in style. Their gentle nature and diplomacy wins them many loyal friends. Their agreeable and peaceful dispositions make them an asset to any family, friendship or business that is fortunate enough to enjoy them. Whites are typically moderate people without the extremes of other personalities. Like the water they represent, they flow over and around life's difficulties rather than demanding that obstacles in their path be moved. Their leadership is solid and fair. They tolerate differences and encourage camaraderie with all team members. The chameleon is their trademark and reflects their ability to adapt and blend with everyone. They enjoy the enviable strength of balance. They are receptive to every personality and willingly learn from all of them. Whites are most effective at putting life's crises in proper perspective. Satisfied and even-tempered, they ask little of life. They often enjoy the protection of stronger personalities. Patient and tolerant, they have much to give. And give they do, with gentle approval for those fortunate enough to experience their accepting embrace.

White Strengths

AS AN INDIVIDUAL

- quiet, reflective and peaceful
- sincere and genuine lifestyle
- appears to accept life comfortably
- patient with self and others
- enjoys life's simplicity
- compatible with others
- kind to animals and people
- blendable in all situations

AS A COMMUNICATOR

- receptive to other's input
- negotiator and mediator on issues
- listens superbly
- strong empathy skills

AS A GOAL SETTER

- receptive to suggestions
- appreciates exposure to many possibilities
- recognizes the value of goal-setting
- trusts self to succeed in many different environments

AS A CAREER PERSON

- accommodates others easily
- handles bureaucratic environments well
- negotiates well
- calm under pressure
- prefers slower pace and "think" time
- sometimes puts self in dangerous occupations for excitement
- non-conformist

AS A PARENT

- flows well with crisis
- takes time to enjoy each child

- agreeable with difficult children
- respected by children for gentle manner and style
- slow to react with anger
- supportive and considerate
- accepts companion's decisions—demonstrates unity
- patient with deviant and inappropriate behavior
- accepts differences superbly

AS A CHILD

- very agreeable to established traditions and boundaries
- non-demanding
- willing to accommodate siblings and parents
- plays well by self
- accepts life with drama

AS A FRIEND

- patient and enduring through good and bad times
- tolerant of unkind behavior
- supportive and accepting
- listens with empathy
- relaxed in most situations
- liked by most people
- compatible with various different personalities
- likes most people
- enjoys observing others
- non-demanding of friendship

AS A COMMITTED COMPANION

- tolerant of other's tardiness
- can entertain self easily
- appreciates leadership qualities in others
- loyal and committed to relationship
- willing to accept beliefs and values of companion

CAREERS MOST LIKELY TO ATTRACT WHITES

Forest Ranger	Recreation Leader	Veterinarian
Dentist	Researcher	Lawyer
Bureaucrat	Homemaker	Engineer
Computer Programmer	Police Officer	F.B.I. Agent
Military Service	Preschool Teacher	Truck Driver

Note: White and Yellows are usually the least motivated to succeed in the career world.

PERSONALITIES WHO APPEAR TO BE POSITIVE WHITES

President George Bush	Albert Einstein	Jimmy Carter

WHITE NATIONS

Finland	Switzerland	Canada

White Limitations

AS AN INDIVIDUAL

- boring and detached
- takes passive approach to life
- unresponsive or openly excited about experiences
- has problems becoming intimate
- bashful and unsure of self
- easily manipulated in changing plans
- ambivilant about direction and goals to pursue
- often lazy and unwilling to take responsibility for self
- non-descript
- resists making commitments

AS A COMMUNICATOR

- fearful of confrontation
- unable to verbally respond quickly in conversation
- dishonest with feelings—often agrees only to please others

- hesitant to engage others in conversation
- doesn't contribute openly
- accepts other's decisions without seeking best solution
- gives very little energy to conversation unless forced
- refuses to take a stand on issues
- prefers to observe other's interact

AS A GOAL SETTER

- takes a "wait and see" attitude to life experiences
- waits for a sign or someone else to make decisions for them
- lacks consistency with goal setting
- sees goals as demanding and therefore restrictive
- waits for others to set his or her goals and then criticizes the goals set for him or her

AS A CAREER PERSON

- low profile
- low energy
- directionless—requires leadership from others
- resents harsh direction and leadership from others
- works at a slower pace
- resists power dominance of other personalities
- difficult to motivate and inspire
- willing to stay in same, monotonous job
- fears change and risk-taking
- easily manipulated by others when unmotivated or unconcerned

AS A PARENT

- refuses to engage in conflict with spouse about children
- doesn't initiate activities and interaction with children
- poor disciplinarian
- works obsessively to maintain peace
- poor leadership and delegation with children
- easily abused by children when promoting unpopular ideas
- easily controlled or ignored by spouse or children

AS A CHILD

- resents being pressured to do things
- doesn't contribute much to conversations
- waits for parent to initiate ideas and then criticizes unacceptable suggestions
- easily ignored
- prefers the comforts of home to the demands of the world
- indifferent to family dilemmas
- doesn't complete tasks
- contributes only in silent manner
- uninvolved in family action

AS A FRIEND

- lacks creativity for making suggestions
- easily led by other's opinions
- won't express honest perception if controversial
- passive
- requires extra protection and a lot of support
- easily hurt and defeated

AS A COMMITTED COMPANION

- prefers the other person to lead
- boring and indecisive
- too accommodating
- won't make suggestions for activities
- willing to let life and love pass him or her by
- may experience difficulty initiating relationships
- feels too inadequate to take a stand and voice opinions
- not emotional about intimate relationships

How to Develop a Positive Connection with Whites

Do:

1. Be loving and sensitive
2. Be firm

3. Provide a structure (boundaries) for them to operate in
4. Be patient and gentle
5. Introduce options and ideas for their involvement
6. Be simple and open
7. Accept their individuality
8. Be casual, informal and relaxed
9. Look for non-verbal clues to their feelings
10. Listen quietly

Don't:

1. Be unkind
2. Expect them to always need others to play with
3. Force verbal expression
4. Be domineering
5. Be too intense
6. Overwhelm them with too much
7. Force confrontation
8. Speak too fast
9. Take away their day dreams
10. Demand leadership

CHAPTER SEVEN

Yellows: The Fun Lovers

Happy and Fun

Riding on the primary motive of fun, Yellows reflect the spirit of the wind and the life-giving miracle of fresh air. They are as essential to society as breathing is to the human existence. Yellows love life. They are spirited, exciting and have an innate ability to be happy. They have a mental attitude which allows them to appreciate what they have rather than be miserable about what they lack. Fate often appears to smile on them and they are considered to be very close friends with "lady luck."

Self-Centered and Uncommitted

Equally affected by the primary motive of fun, Yellows exemplify the ultimate "light-weight" personality. Yellows bound through life well-focused on themselves. They frequently fail to develop the depth necessary to contribute substantially to society. Yellows struggle to understand why anyone would rather "earn their keep" than take the easy road through life. Perhaps their most serious limitation is their lack of commitment. Despite their enthusiasm, Yellows start more projects than any other group and successfully complete the least. (Typical of Yellows, one patient complained that she had started three hundred ninety-four diets in a one year period consisting of three hundred sixty-five days.)

Commitment requires constant dedication which unduly taxes a Yellow's capacity for endurance. They usually cannot concentrate long enough to convince others that their intentions are genuine and trustworthy. One young man was unable to commit to marriage and repeatedly broke engagements and women's hearts. He was completely overwhelmed by the thought of a life-long commitment. He enjoyed the romance but feared the expectations of a committed relationship. Eventually he fell so deeply in love that he felt motivated to consider the possibility of marriage. However, his endurance failed him once again and he called his father for consolation. He respected his father and listened to his wise counsel. His father knew his son's fear of commitment was creating his difficulty, but he also knew the young man had a fine character. The father simply reminded him that divorce was always an option and if necessary he could always exercise that option in the future.

This wise father offered his Yellow son an escape route to marry. He provided the essential ingredient in every Yellow's life—an escape—an out—a chance to run away, if necessary. His wisdom and effective parenting brought his son and wife together. Happily, my wife and I celebrated our twelfth wedding anniversary this year.

Equally difficult is committing to personal development. Getting to know oneself is a difficult task for everyone. Yellows often give up before they really tackle new issues in their psychological make-up. Commitment to painful soul searching usually ends up way down on their list of priorities. Yellows are unwilling to pay the price for true self-confidence which can only come from a lifetime of commitments to those experiences, people and values one cherishes. Yellows go with the flow of traffic as long as it is flowing and flashy. They love excitement and willingly forego the discomfort of commitment in order to feel momentary pleasure.

Irresponsible

While society has come up with some wonderful adjectives to describe Yellows (some of which I can't even put in this book), the word that most accurately describes the negative essence of the Yellow personality is "irresponsible." Remember that wonderful song, "Call me unreliable... call me undependable?" Save yourself some time and simply call them Yellow.

Yellows have a most difficult time accepting responsibility for themselves. Somehow they truly believe taking care of them is someone else's responsibility. It doesn't matter who—just someone else. After all, since no one is having the fun they are having, what could they possibly be doing that is more important than concerning themselves with the needs of the Yellows?! Perhaps the greatest concern with Yellows is their loss of quality time in life. They can be "cute" with their rebellious natures while still young, but society has little tolerance for adult bums. There is perhaps nothing more tragic than an aging Yellow without character. Their faces bear the heavy lines from year-round tans on the ski slopes. Their personal belongings are often minimal because they have never concerned themselves with proper care for them. They have few intimate friends. Yellows often take the easy path and in the end, the easy path is filled with soft dirt that buckles under the burdensome emptiness and dependency of the Yellow's life.

Their irresponsible nature and inability to commit often make "taming" Yellows seem like one is pursuing the impossible dream. They are typically so charismatic that others fail to see their limitations. Only after a period of time, do they see Yellows for what they often are—a beautiful, prancing, race horse who rarely goes the distance. After committing time and energy to this exciting performer, the owner is eventually disenchanted with his expectations and often feels anger and regret at having believed in his capacity to change this "Yellow" race horse into a durable plow horse who will go the distance in a relationship. In other words, achieving the impossible dream.

Yellows do not feel comfortable with the pressures that often come with being responsible. One patient told her Yellow husband, "If I weren't around, you would probably be lighting candles every night rather than remembering to pay your electric bill." After talking with them for a short time, I was certain that she was right. He had neglected to pay the last three months $525 mortgage payment so they decided to sell the home and now rent a small apartment for $400 a month. He further justified this poor business thinking by saying, "All I need is a place with a little land for my dog and she can have a horse. Other than that I just want to travel. In fact, if I had my way, we would load up the van right now and go live in Mexico for a while."

We further discussed the need for more stability in raising children and providing a secure environment for his Blue wife. He told me he had already matured because when he first met her, all he did was cash his paycheck each week, deposit it in his back pocket, and enjoy life until he reached in his back pocket and found all the money was gone. Then he would just sit around the house or bum off buddies until he earned his next paycheck. Like most Yellows, life is for today and saving money is for those who don't know how to live today. They have a very hard time putting off until tomorrow what can be done today as long as it is fun. They philosophize that working is for people who don't know how to party.

Blaming others is a classic pattern for irresponsible Yellows. I was working with one young man (Rob) who wept when we discussed his Red father and the non-existent relationship they had. After two sessions he was much less rebellious and making substantial progress until one day he confessed that he had stolen his father's bank card and withdrawn over eight hundred and fifty dollars in the last three months. Once involved, he didn't know how to stop or tell anyone. At last he had been discovered and would have to face his father, whom he despised. With his mother attentively listening in my office, the young man spent fifteen minutes explaining why he could never tell his father because his father wouldn't understand. I knew Rob always excused his delinquent behavior in school and home by using his father as a scapegoat. Now he had stolen his father's money, and spent it all frivolously on himself, and still he wanted his mother and me to excuse him because his father was (in Rob's eyes) a "terrible" man. For years Rob hadn't wanted to change himself, so he simply explained away his truancies, failing grades, lack of friends, and now, *stealing,* on the inadequacies of his father.

One Yellow patient in her mid-twenties spent her life telling everyone how boring and old-fashioned her parents were. She justified her negative attitude by reminding others how unsuccessful her parents were financially and that they didn't communicate well between themselves. She found hundreds of reasons why she would rather die than live their lifestyle. Therapy continued off and on for about one year before she finally began to see that rather than responsibly focusing on her personal growth, she continually spent an enormous amount of energy on her "frumpy old parents who knew nothing about living." She began to recognize that she had actually produced very little in her own life. She had completed only three credits of college. She had never sustained a meaningful relationship with a man. She had been unable to lose any weight for the period of one year. Her friends were exactly like her. She was in debt up to her ears with no sign of change. She had not held a job for longer than five months. It all came crushing in on her like a tidal wave when I reminded her that she had discontinued therapy, in part due to financial strain and that her "frumpy old parents who knew nothing about living" had approached me and offered to help pay for my services if I felt it would help her. She had maligned them both her entire life. Yet, they knew enough about real living to offer assistance to their daughter without any strings attached.

She finally broke down and expressed her self-hate. She did not want a boring life like her parents, but she realized that she had been totally ineffective in building a more positive lifestyle for herself. She had produced nothing while attacking them. She acknowledged that she only loved herself when she performed and produced. Yet, she was so undisciplined and irresponsible that she had only known repeated failure in life. She had great talents and numerous interests but, as yet, had been unwilling to look at herself, and then commit to anything long enough to experience the joy which comes from responsible effort.

Too many Yellow married individuals explain away having affairs on the insensitivity of their spouse. "If she or he were more willing to enjoy sex with me, then I wouldn't have to do this." Of course, they fail to recognize that often the reason their spouse doesn't enjoy sex may be due to their lack of commitment or other shortcomings. Instead, Yellows find places to put their blame and move on through life, carelessly avoiding any responsibility for having to look at or change themselves. This irresponsible nature could be remedied much easier if Yellows had a sense of conscience or guilt, but neither accompanies Yellows very far on their journey through life. Believing that customs are only relevant when they serve the needs for the individual, Yellows may too freely abandon tradition in favor of personal gratification, regardless of its long-term consequences.

Enthusiastic and Carefree

Yellows seek enchanting opportunities and find life laced with silver linings. They rarely become bogged down with details or "emotional baggage." "Emotional baggage" comes in the form of controlling friends, poor work conditions and other undersirable and demanding circumstances. Yellows are as vulnerable to these experiences as any personality, but they have a strong yearning for freedom and subconsciously recognize baggage and instinctively move away from its influence.

Yellows represent enthusiasm and share this excitement with everyone they meet. They are terrific at social involvements and have a sixth sense for making a party out of everyday living. They remind us of our youth and the joy which comes from innocent hopes and optimistic dreams.

Playful and Exciting

Yellows enjoy life regardless of what they are doing. Even when working hard, Yellows appear to be having a good time. Their lives are filled with confidence that the best is yet to come. They have a zest for living which is contagious. A Blue individual called a Yellow friend long distance after five years of silence and said, "I've missed the life we shared as friends in college. You always seemed to make life happen for me. I often reflect back on our friendship and remember all the excitement you always stirred up. I miss you because you breathed life into me." The Yellow friend had no idea that he had been the instigator of all the fun. He naively assumed that everyone's primary goal in life was to have a good time. He also thought most people experienced life as freely and comfortably as he did. Later in life, he learned that his was a unique and enviable style which Yellows come to life with and continue to cultivate wherever they go. They seem to know how to make life fun regardless of their circumstances.

No personality plays like Yellows. They are so spontaneous that they are always ready for whatever fun opportunities come their way. Yellows are easy marks for a good time. They often find themselves sporting T-shirts with colorful slogans like, "Are we having fun yet?" and "It's OK to PLAY." They do not need to be productive with their play. The activity of play is, in itself, value enough to warrant a Yellow's attention.

Yellows love surprises. They love to celebrate everything imaginable. They find holidays and special moments refreshing and, barring a memory lapse (which they are noted for), they will make the most of every opportunity to have fun.

Superficial

Ski resorts, beaches, amusement parks and other magical environments are filled with Yellows seeking the good life without a price. One of my first professional experiences was working with youth in Park City, Utah. At that time, Park City was a sleepy little hole in the wall comprised of one elementary school and a secondary school. The families primarily ranged from the low to middle socioeconomic class. In fact, some of the kid's parents were left over coal miners from the "good old days." Imagine the task I faced in trying to convince these young people that in the long run, a life of stability and commitment was far more promising than the momentary pleasures of playing on the ski slopes all season, complete with too much drinking, too many drugs and too casual sex. The full time ski enthusiasts were gorgeous, trim, smiling, and carefree imitators of happiness. Compare them to the parents of these young people who popped popcorn at night and sweated over how to come up with next month's mortgage. The young people were torn dramatically between the playful, carefree world many Yellows espouse and the real world where personal responsibility and concern for others provides a foundation for rewarding lifestyles.

Yellows may suffer from lack of personal integrity for the good of others. They enjoy the company of others but often find themselves unwilling to commit beyond the pleasures of momentary good times. Yellows resist activities or people requiring endurance which limits them from perhaps the greatest goals of all—high self-esteem based on earned productivity and deep intimacy only experienced in long-term committed relationships.

Disorganized and Incomplete

Yellows would like to change. In fact, they prefer change. However, *what* they change is usually unimportant and *when* they change is often counterproductive. One Yellow friend lamented that every time he had a big project coming due, he would clean his garage instead. Rather than focus on the essential projects, he wasted hours focusing on irrelevant puttering. Equally frustrating was his inability to organize effectively, even leaving his garage in a constant state of disruption rather than order. When he would finally tackle the essential project, he would be forced to toss it together instead of preparing a quality presentation. Within himself, he felt incomplete as if he was almost cheating himself and others from the best quality performance that he was capable of.

Yellows learn early in life to cut the corners. They often claim credit for accomplishments not yet fully achieved. They simply tell half-truths or feel it isn't that big of a deal whether they are what they say as long as it doesn't hurt anyone.

Life has a way of providing natural consequences for our behaviors. In other words, you reap what you sow. Many Yellows are so talented and would love the applause of others. Yet, they are unwilling to put in the time and effort to earn the praise they seek.

Impulsive and Undisciplined

Yellows often display flighty and undisciplined dispositions. They are terribly restless and find sticking with any task quite boring. Yellows often experience numerous job changes—not because jobs are uninteresting, but because the Yellows generally become uninterested. Yellows believe life should be experienced in the fast lane if it's going to be experienced at all.

Yellows are impulsive and restless. One can never be sure what to expect from these unpredictable individuals. Here today, gone to Maui! They are quick to change but often unproductive in the changing process. It is hard to hang on to these flighty Yellows who constantly seek the free and easy life. They know how to have a good time and wish everyone else would work to make that possible.

One Yellow man purchased a new video camera for Christmas and let it sit in the box for a week before his friend happened to drop by and notice it. His friend had the best time figuring out where to connect things and how to use the zoom lens. The camera owner was momentarily intrigued until his friend recommended that he read the instruction book himself so he could use the camera effectively. Weeks later, after the Yellow's wife pressed him repeatedly to remember to bring the camera on various occasions, he realized he couldn't continue to play stupid so he innocently announced that the camera didn't work right anymore. It was brilliant manipulation. He knew his Blue wife couldn't accept a broken camera sitting around the house when they had paid so much money for it. He also knew that she wouldn't return the camera until she tried to fix it herself. Within a matter of two hours, she had mastered the camera and became the official photographer for the rest of their marriage. Yellows prefer not to be bothered with the details of life. They simply want the praise for what they do accomplish and the credit for whatever commitments they miraculously maintain in their life.

Yellows are very interested in the details and patience necessary for preserving wildlife. They are always ready to throw a party. Daily routine quickly becomes monotonous and Yellows slip away into new and different environments. They hate exercise unless they can socialize at the same time or watch themselves in a mirror. Yellows find amazing excuses for not disciplining themselves. Once their excuses fail them, and society imposes restrictions on them, be prepared for sullen, angry behavior.

Anger is never experienced when one is powerful. Anger is expressed due to one's powerlessness in any given situation. Yellows often express anger when life becomes difficult and unfair. They feel instant frustration when problems aren't easily solved. Subsequently, few Yellows ever become chief executive officers or powerful leaders. (President Ronald Reagan is the exception.) They are not interested in power and even if they were, finding the dedication to stay with a challenging dilemma would quickly discourage them. Fixing things when they lack the necessary skill to do so infuriates Yellows. Daily activities like driving on busy freeways, balancing checkbooks, putting oil in the car, looking up phone numbers in a telephone directory, etc., can upset Yellows so easily that they often lose their concentration and begin immediately rummaging through their mind for escapes from this insanity others call "responsible living."

Charismatic and Popular

Yellows find it easy to relate with people of all ages. They make friends with all the kids on their block where they live. They charm elderly people in stores and babies in strollers with their entertaining style. They reflect a joyful nature that entices many of those whom they encounter to brighten their own disposition.

Yellows often appear to be very attractive people. They have the most engaging style of all the personalities. A descriptive adjective commonly attributed to Yellows is charismatic. They parent charismatically. They conduct business charismatically. They converse charismatically. Often considered the pied pipers of humanity, Yellows can easily move groups of people to tears and/or laughter.

Yellows love to entertain and be entertained. They often stage productions in the garage for other neighborhood children, run for student body offices in school, and choose careers where they have a great amount of exposure to people. They give freely of themselves. Perhaps because they crave their own freedom so dearly, Yellows do not seek to control others. They live without many expectations and give without concern for what they might receive.

They are often the "life of the party" in social settings. Yellows find laughter and interpersonal relationships easy to experience. They sincerely like people and typically find themselves surrounded by friends. They are very popular in most environments without ever having to seek social acceptance. Their trusting nature draws other personalities toward them. People sense their innocent and trusting nature. Yellows are typically very open, which makes their friendship easy to understand and maintain. Yellows usually enjoy a carefree lifestyle. Other personalities seek out Yellow friends because of their positive and cheerful manner.

Naive and Trusting

No personality experiences life as naively trusting as Yellows. They don't think things through in their minds prior to speaking or doing. I remember working with Jennifer (fifteen years old) and her Red mother shortly following Jennifer being raped. The mother was so angry she could hardly talk about her daughter's ordeal. Yet, Jennifer felt little concern over the experience. She explained that an older man (approximately 40 years old) and a woman stopped to ask directions and eventually asked if she would be interested in modeling for a magazine. She consented. (Remember the vanity of Yellows.) The man proceeded to take her and the woman to a shopping center where the woman explained that she needed to pick up a few things from the store. Jennifer accompanied the man to a back alleyway where he proceeded to rape her. She didn't like the experience, but cooperated and even asked for a ride part way home because it was too far to walk. Her mother suffered the consequences of the rape far longer than Jennifer did. However, not all Yellows can accept the consequences of their naivety like Jennifer.

Yellows often find themselves victims of their own naivete. They are easily fooled and easy prey for more sophisticated and calculating personalities. They trust easily and yet, often build high walls to prevent intimacy once sufficient emotional scarring occurs.

Yellows are not particularly bothered by broken commitments such as appointments, but broken emotional commitments can be devastating. Yellows may get stuck in superficial relationships when they have been bitterly hurt. This is particularly unfortunate since deep inside they are driven by intimacy. Subsequently, they deny themselves one of their greatest needs because of "imagined" or real broken promises in their lives. It is not uncommon to see misguided, superficial Yellows floating through life as if they prefer their freedom to intimacy, but it typically comes from earlier scars or distrust. Since Blues are known for their sincerity and loyalty, this may, at least in part, explain why Yellows often seek their companionship.

Chatter-Box and Flip

Yellows are often nicknamed "chatter-box." Yellows can usually find *anything* interesting enough to talk about. This is usually helpful in the dating scene but can be quite stressful for colleagues and family members. When idle chatter is combined with rude and loud behavior, Yellows are considered obnoxious. This label always offends them because they can't comprehend why anyone wouldn't find them as delightful and entertaining as they find themselves.

One distressed mother feared she would gag her four year old child if something didn't change soon. She was so tired of non-stop conversation that she admittedly stopped listening simply to save her own sanity. (Personally, I think she was also concerned for the child's life.) She liked her quiet time, and everytime she simply sat down in order to gather her thoughts, her daughter pounced on her lap and tried to cheer her up. The mother actually hid from her at times throughout the day so that she might enjoy some peace.

The conversational approach to life is also frustrating when you want to be serious, and Yellows don't, can't or won't. "Just once," a desperate husband lamented, "could my wife listen and feel my pain without making a joke out of everything?! Not everything belongs in the Sunday funnies. I can't begin to tell you the number of times I have held my feelings inside because I knew she would make light of something I felt more serious about." So goes the irritation of communicating deeply with a light-hearted Yellow.

When totally left to themselves, Yellows often take a flippant, rude and self-centered approach to others in the family. They are often socially adept and poke fun at other family members who lack the necessary social skills to defend themselves. They are notorious for interrupting conversations whether you are busy or not. Nothing is sacred to the Yellow and they are equally certain that nothing is sacred to others. Whether you are on the telephone or reading, Yellows will find a way of distracting you until you acknowledge their needs. This often infuriates those who accompany Yellows through life. When you add up all the small irritations of Yellows it can be quite disconcerting to encounter them. They are loud show-offs willing to embarrass anyone for a good-natured laugh. They interrupt without hesitation feeling that nothing is so important that it can't wait for them. They talk constantly as if words were the music of life. They regard themselves as cute and entertaining. Quick-witted (and quick-tongued), Yellows can toss sarcastic bombs with expertise only rivaled by Reds. Their vanity and self-centered natures can wear obnoxiously after a lengthy period of time. They can be an intolerable force to deal with in the social realm.

Yellow Limitations

Yellows have little regard for the property of others. They are sloppy and messy individuals who keep themselves clean and polished while their homes often suffer from neglect. They want to look particularly good to the world and when social praise is a consideration they are quick to comply with society's standards. Otherwise, cleanliness may be too much effort to compel them to show much concern.

They are disorganized in their environments and personal thoughts. Rather than focusing on real issues and important events, Yellows putter with minor concerns and irrelevant activity much of their life. They have a difficult time committing to anything which takes priority over play time and consequently find themselves somewhat superficial and empty with regards to relationships.

Yellow Strengths

Despite their struggle with self-discipline and commitment, Yellows are eager to experience all facets of life. They naively call for the spotlight to be placed on them as they play out their life as though it were center stage. Yellows are our constant reminder that youth is in the eye of the beholder.

They are constantly youthful in their attitudes towards new ideas, change, relationships, occupations and the future. Yellows carry that childlike quality of hope that inspires the masses to appreciate and value themselves as well as the wonderful world in which they live. Yellows promote the good in others and willingly ignore their limitations. Yellows are more inclined to like themselves just for what "they are" rather than what "they do." They are the people connectors and the social glue of society. Yellows express themselves candidly and genuinely. They give playful attention to living and inspire others to do the same. Freely, they offer their opinions as well as themselves, often spreading a contagious spirit of friendship wherever they go. Once your life has been intimately touched by a Yellow, you will more fully appreciate the incredible joy achievable by the human soul and optimistic hope attainable within the human heart.

Yellow Strengths

AS AN INDIVIDUAL

- highly optimistic (rarely depressed)
- likes self and accepts others easily
- loves to volunteer for opportunities
- sees life as an experience to be enjoyed
- flashy and spunky (race horse rather than plow horse)
- adventurous and daring

AS A COMMUNICATOR

- spontaneous thinker (quick on his or her feet)
- enjoys and promotes being physical (hugs, touching)
- easy to converse with
- comfortable with people
- able to express self directly in conflict
- energized by large groups
- superb at superficial conversation

AS A GOAL SETTER

- appreciates and lives for the present

- prioritizes play time first
- very flexible
- accepts guidance from others
- disciplined if he or she finds the task fun and challenging
- demands action versus observation

AS A CAREER PERSON

- people-oriented
- friendly
- able to take risks
- high energy
- inspires colleagues and subordinates to cooperate and excel
- charismatic and enjoyable to work with
- breaks up monotony of work world with personal highlights
- likes to tackle short term projects with visible results
- enjoys dressing up and also comfortable with casual attire
- supports dreams and intuitive thinking

AS A PARENT

- highly entertaining
- promotes fun family activities
- excellent short term leader
- finds touching children natural and comfortable
- flows easily with negative experiences
- turns crisis into comedy
- non-judgmental of children's friends
- children enjoy their company and seek them out
- concern themselves with broad picture rather than details

AS A CHILD

- fun to have around
- playful and entertaining
- enjoys new experiences
- accepting of differences
- loves to socialize (brings friends around the house)

- easily approached with communication
- strong visual learner
- loves physical contact (hugging, kissing)
- pliable—willing to bend in order to please
- curious and inquisitive

AS A FRIEND

- vulnerable, innocent and trusting
- endearing
- exciting and fun to be with (never dull or boring)
- often prioritizes friends over family (or at least equally)
- forgiving of self and others
- lively and entertaining
- willing to free up schedule in order to play

AS A COMMITTED COMPANION

- brings excitement to spouse
- promotes intimacy with a creative flare
- enjoys unusual experiences
- not burdened with emotional strings
- few expectations of others
- agreeable to change
- accepts other's suggestions

CAREERS MOST LIKELY TO ATTRACT YELLOWS

Firefighter	Beautician	Secretary
International Consultant	Entertainer	Drama/Acting
Travel Agent	Tour Guide	Sales
Recreation Leader	Circus Performer	Retail
Lifeguard	Insurance Agent	Clergy/Minister

Note: Yellows are generally least capable of committing to the career world.

PERSONALITIES WHO APPEAR TO BE POSITIVE YELLOWS

Ronald Reagan	Goldie Hawn	John F. Kennedy
	and Me!!!	

YELLOW NATIONS

Mexico   Australia   Brazil

Yellow Limitations

AS AN INDIVIDUAL

- irresponsible and unreliable
- self-centered and egotistical
- flighty and uncommitted
- lots of talk with little action
- superficial and mostly interested in a good time
- unwilling to experience pain in order to produce quality
- undisciplined
- loud and obnoxious in public places
- needs to look good socially (high priority)
- exaggerates stories and omits unpleasant truths
- unable to confront or face issues

AS A COMMUNICATOR

- often speaks before thinking
- unsympathetic towards depression in others
- makes insensitive jokes about serious and sensitive issues
- lightminded and superficial
- often repetitious
- interrupts others freely
- forgets what others tell them
- overly dramatic in expressing self (often uses superlatives)
- often talks too much about everything and nothing
- poor listener

AS A GOAL SETTER

- terribly undisciplined in committing to goals
- prefers to play today rather than plan for tomorrow
- feels no need to prepare for the future
- restless and finds it difficult to stick with long term goals

- more interested in "appearing on stage" than "writing the script"
- disorganized and scattered in too many directions

AS A CAREER PERSON

- requires fun in all activities
- can handle stress for only short periods of time
- poor concentration for any length of time
- unwilling to dedicate self to a cause without vacations
- resents authority and defiant to leaders
- sloppy and unpredictable
- needs a lot of interaction with people
- takes few things seriously

AS A PARENT

- self-centered and concerned about self before children's needs
- can be sarcastic with children
- unwilling to spend a lot of time and energy on children's behalf
- inconsistent with discipline
- more interested in enjoying children than teaching them
- irresponsible and too permissive with children
- doesn't role model positive work habits
- lacks discipline for house cleaning or stable income

AS A CHILD

- sassy and demanding
- defiant to authority
- forgetful of assignments and parental expectations
- more concerned with friends than family
- teases siblings constantly
- insensitive to parent responsibilities or needs
- prefers to take the easy road whenever possible
- shows little initiative for family concerns and responsibilities
- unconcerned with financial issues

AS A FRIEND

- spends most of time discussing self and his/her life

- shows up at his or her convenience
- undependable in crisis
- pursues own life regardless of friend's situation or needs
- unwilling to commit to long term needs of distressed friends
- uncomfortable in painful or distressing environments
- disloyal to friendships—makes new friends easily and without guilt

AS A COMMITTED COMPANION

- uncommitted and flighty in long term relationships
- undependable and inconsiderate of other's needs
- prefers knowing there is an escape to every relationship
- unwilling to "hang in there" with the difficult times
- quick-tempered in unpleasant circumstances requiring patience
- unwilling to invest time in personal growth to improve relationships
- capable of ignoring the feelings of others and focusing on self

How to Develop a Positive Relationship with Yellows

Do:

1. Be positive
2. Adore them
3. Touch them physically
4. Accept their playful teasing
5. Remember they are tender
6. Praise them
7. Remember they hold feelings deeply
8. Promote playful activities for and with them
9. Enjoy their charismatic innocence
10. Allow them opportunity for verbal expression

Don't:

1. Be too serious or sober in criticism
2. Push them too intensely
3. Ignore them
4. Forget they have "down" times also
5. Demand perfection
6. Expect them to dwell on problems
7. Give them too much rope or they may hang themselves
8. Classify them as "just" lightweight social butterflies
9. Attack their sensitivity
10. Totally control their schedules

CHAPTER EIGHT

Character: How To Become Your Best Color

Character is a powerful phenomenon with complex beginnings. We can explain personality as innate, but character defies such a simple explanation. Our understanding of character begins with an accurate definition.

Let's picture ourselves as large computers. We have been programmed to develop and produce certain data. Depending on our programming, we will each present a unique style of data. This is our personality. It allows us to present what we have been programmed to do. We are limited to whatever our programmer has designed for us.

Now let's look at the large black button on our computer. This is the OVERRIDE BUTTON. Pushing this button at any time allows us to negate, develop or change any data in our computer, whether we have been previously programmed with the desired capability or not. It is our way of designing data we prefer. It enables us to override our predetermined data. This is character development. It is the new software that allows for new and rewarding experiences.

It is character, when a Red personality *tolerates* differences, or a Blue personality takes time to *play,* or a White personality *asserts* himself or herself as a leader, or a Yellow personality *commits* to an intimate relationship. When we push our black OVERRIDE button, these behaviors go against the natural grain of our innate personality and require developed character in order to exist.

Individuals develop character strengths and limitations just as they have innate personality strengths and limitations. Furthermore, it appears that some character traits are most innately compatible with certain personalities. There are obvious strengths and limitations which every individual must deal with from birth. Though we may not be born with a particular character trait, we do appear to be more receptive and/or vulnerable to certain strengths and limitations based on our given personality color.

Consider the SEVEN MOST COMMON CHARACTER STRENGTHS OF EACH COLOR.

RED	BLUE	WHITE	YELLOW
loyalty to task	loyalty to people	tolerant	accepting
committed	committed	patience	forgiving
directed	quality	cooperation	friendly
logical	sincere	relaxed	optimistic
leadership	honest	understanding	trusting
focused	focused	balanced	appreciative
proactive	moral conscience	obedient	receptive

There are also SEVEN MOST COMMON CHARACTER LIMITATIONS OF EACH COLOR.

RED	BLUE	WHITE	YELLOW
pride (arrogance)	self-righteous	uncommitted	uncommitted
insensitive	judgmental	stubborn	insensitive
poor listener	easily depressed	dishonest	obnoxious
tactless	controlling	lazy	irresponsible
rebellious	unforgiving	uninvolved	rebellious
critical of others	suspicious	dependent	self-centered
impatient	illogical	directionless	permissive

Character, not personality, is the predominant factor in ultimately determining the quality of our lives. Character is essentially anything we learn to think, feel or do that is initially unnatural and requires effort to develop. Character is reflected with the changes we make in our values and beliefs through our lives.

Factors Affecting Character Development

There are several components which are essential to character development. The first component is (1) IDENTIFYING POSITIVE LIFE PRINCIPLES. Life principles are Universal Truths. Universal Truths are those truths common to everyone. Universal Truths may include loving and being loved, the need for food and shelter, or the importance of feeling there is purpose in our lives. Universal Truths may be theoretical or philosophical in nature. These Truths help us to become more effective and charactered. They include the knowledge that:

- Every person can offer unique strengths to a relationship.

- Individuals with personal confidence feel little need for power plays with others

- People that like themselves find it easier to like and accept others than do those who feel inadequate

- When we spend energy belittling others and blocking their development, we limit ourselves from growing

Universal Truths become life principles when we proactively pursue and live them. Life principles enhance our color by giving us insight into how others perceive things differently from us. These same life principles assist us in overcoming our inherent personality limitations by developing uncomfortable, yet, positive attitudes and behaviors based on Universal Truths.

By comparison, personal truths differ from Universal Truths in their focus. Personal truths may include careers we choose, friends we enjoy, hobbies we pursue, or the amount of sleep time we require. Personal truths are those unique and healthy lifestyles we individually prefer, regardless of our personality color. When we think *everyone* should drive fast or slow on the freeway, we cause accidents. When we think *everyone* should be academically educated, we deprive our skilled laborers of earned self-respect.

Some of us would be miserable if we were psychotherapists or medical doctors. Others would be miserable as plumbers or auto mechanics. Unfortunately, we may disguise our own professional and personal insecurities by criticizing the occupations of others. We think this gives our occupations more prestige. Personal truths suggest that one occupation is not necessarily better than another as long as both render an honest service. CHARACTERED INDIVIDUALS UNDERSTAND THIS CONCEPT. SIMPLE, INNATE PERSONALITIES DO NOT. We can waste so much energy trying to force *personal truths* into *Universal Truths*. We develop character when we identify *Universal Truths* and embrace them. We also foster effective human relationships when we understand and accept others in light of their *personal truths*.

The second component of character building is (2) FREE WILL. *If free will were not at the core of our very human existence, we would be subjected to the limitations of our innate personalities from birth.* There would be no personal development or possibility for change. Developing our character is a process whereby we can balance our personalities. Without character building, we must remain unfulfilled and limited. Developing our character allows us to more fully enjoy an exciting and productive life.

Character is usually shaped best in an atmosphere of free will. Free will lies at the root of every healthy character building program. One young woman was forced to practice piano every morning for two hours before school. She appeared very charactered to those who witnessed this daily ritual. However, healthy character is reflected by consistent commitment to positive Universal Truths (life principles). This young woman grew to hate the piano. She also hated her father who demanded that she practice so often. She even hated herself for allowing him to control her life. Unfortunately, she had developed unhealthy character by committing to the negative motive of pleasing others at all costs and resenting and blaming everyone for her miserable life in the process. Similarly, her father had erred in demanding that his daughter develop character by working on his values rather her own. He was shocked when she attempted multiple suicides, voiced her hatred for him, confessed that she was bulimic, and vowed never to play the piano again. Neither the father nor the daughter had effectively identified positive Universal Truths (life principles) and consistently committed themselves to them. Both had accepted unhealthy character. When we accept another's personal truths as our Universal Truths, we are giving up our freedom of choice and limiting our growth.

The third component of character building is (3) OTHER HUMAN INFLUENCES IN OUR LIVES. We are often told that we preach our greatest sermons by the lives we lead. Example is often all a new born child knows for their first few years of life. As we continue the aging process, we choose examples to follow. After years as a psychotherapist, this writer is convinced that with the exception of self, the most influential factor in childhood character development is the example and influence of parents. As teenagers, we are highly influenced by our peers. As adults, we are most influenced by our spouse. Playing a strong supporting role, however, are siblings, extended family and friends. *We must continually ask ourselves who we seek as role models and who may be looking to us as their model.*

Advantages of Building Character

Character defines the type of positive or negative connection we make with ourselves and others throughout life. Our character is not a casual reality. It is developed over years by personal design and commitment to life principles. Once established, it cannot be easily altered. We must be patient with the process. Character development often takes on numerous twists and changes in its process. However, once the various aspects of character are established, they become as solid as our given personalities at birth.

Knowing that our character will eventually become as solid as our personality should motivate us to enrich ourselves with balanced life experiences. Hopefully we will seek those positive attributes we observe in others through our social interaction. It is the seeking of this balance that eventually provides greater meaning to our own lives.

Many potentially vibrant individuals have allowed themselves to put their best "personality" foot forward rather than presenting a more balanced stance with one "personality" foot and one "character" foot. We are much stronger and valuable when we add to the color of our innate personality by developing the traits of character we observe in others. Once we have identified our existing personality and character traits we can begin to create whatever life-styling image we prefer. I am not suggesting that we alter our innate personality. It is, however, tremendously important for us to constantly strive to develop our character. Personality is the style we use to present our thoughts and actions to others. Character is the core of Universal Truths or Life Principles behind those thoughts and actions we present.

We recognize our flawed human nature. We recognize the many times we have made poor decisions. Yet, we continue to "pick ourselves up" with renewed determination to overcome our limitations. We want our lives to count for something—to matter. We want others to know we have lived for a greater purpose than merely to have survived this existence, after all. This feeling can only come with the developed character. Personality alone can never offer such a powerful sense of destiny.

We have defined character. Now let's look at how each color tends to innately bind our character development. Notice particularly those areas where your personality may be binding another's character. Look for any specific behaviors in any colors that are currently binding your character building process. The following list delineates common and specific ways each personality *binds* the character development of others.

Binding Behaviors

REDS

1. Have a tendency to be overbearing and inflexible (which limits depth of shared feelings and/or perceptions in conversations)

2. Often have exaggerated ego needs (which often creates an unnecessary power struggle)

3. Known to make sarcastic and unkind remarks in order to maintain control (which drives others to a defensive posture when around them)

4. Typically are too task-oriented. They forget the spirit of living and remain too strict in their orientation to life. (If I suggest a Red patient buy flowers for his wife, he may do so, but rarely with the spirit of enjoying it—he completes the letter of the law rather than feeling the spirit of the giving process)

5. Often are judgmental of others' weaknesses (which causes others to hide their insecurities for fear of rejection or ridicule). Doesn't bring out the creative best in others.

6. Tend to resent being questioned and need to always be right. (Typically others learn to lie or pretend they agree with a Red to their face and mock them behind their back.)

7. Often are unappreciative of others. They don't give strokes freely which frustrates others who crave their approval and/or acceptance. This also back-fires on Reds who would enjoy intimacy but rarely get it because they don't generate it themselves.

BLUES

1. Tend to take things too personally (which often causes others to lie in order to protect the insecure and overly sensitive Blue)

2. Often have too many unrealistic expectations (which makes others feel inadequate, unnecessary or unloved)

3. Typically role model lack of self-esteem by placing themselves last on their list of priorities

4. Often are too critical of others who choose to live life with a more relaxed or aggressive style (which causes others to feel unable to ever please them)

5. Tend to be too demanding of other's "inappropriate manners" (which causes others to rebel and develop a dislike for manners altogether)

WHITES

1. May be too easily overwhelmed by life (which causes others to pity whites)

2. Can be too fearful of expressing themselves honestly (which causes others to lose respect for them)

3. Often are too weak to take a stand (which causes others to feel a need to always protect them)

4. Tend to be too insecure to set goals and pursue them (which causes others to resent being held back by their lack of initiative and cooperation in accomplishing joint endeavors)

5. Can be too independent to promote team-work

6. Often are to silently stubborn (which angers others and often causes them to ignore Whites and go their own way)

7. Appear to be too helpless and inadequate (which causes others to want to rescue them)

YELLOWS

1. May appear to be too flighty and uncommitted (which causes people to feel Yellows don't really care about them or anything)

2. Can be too flippant with rude comments (which hurts feelings and/or causes others to not take them seriously)

3. Often are too irresponsible with jobs (which causes others not to trust them to come through)

4. Can be unwilling to learn many living skills (which causes others to lose respect for them or become overprotective of them)

5. Sometimes refuse to accept committed leadership role (which causes others to carry more than their fair share)

6. Can be emotionally dishonest in order to avoid conflict (which causes others to believe things that aren't really happening and/or keeps intimacy on a superficial level)

We have briefly reviewed how the personality limitations of each color actually binds the character development of others. We can easily see the value of building our character. Now we can choose a healthy character building process which will enable us to balance ourselves, and experience the greater meaning life offers to those of us who are willing to reach out and stretch.

How to Build Your Character

In order to build character, we must identify and commit to those Life Principles (Universal Truths) which will maximize our color strengths and minimize the limitations. Regardless of our color, these Life Principles will guide us through the challenging process of character development.

Character building requires attitudinal and behavioral commitments. *Character building must become specific and personal in order to be effective.* For some it may include the act of "letting go" or forgiving another for something that was said or done. For others it may require a physical act such as refusing an alcoholic beverage. It may be initiating a physical embrace with another person. It can be as simple as giving a compliment to a deserving family member or a co-worker.

THE CHARACTER BUILDING PROCESS REQUIRES US TO (1) IDENTIFY HEALTHY LIFE PRINCIPLES, (2) ACCEPT THEM INTO OUR LIVES, (3) COMMIT TO CONSISTENLY LIVING THEM, AND (4) SHARE THEM WITH OTHERS.

Life Principles will benefit all colors in their own development as well as the relationships they encounter with other colors. Key *Life Principles* include:

Life Principle 1

Personal truths must be identified, pursued and blended with Universal Truths in order for us to have a balanced lifestyle.

Life Principle 2

Charactered people take responsibilty for their own attitudes and behaviors.

Life Principle 3

We must stretch and risk personal discomfort in order to make unnatural attitudes and behaviors become natural.

Life Principle 4

Charactered people actively love themselves and others.

Life Principle 5

Our strengths must be shared with others in order to fully benefit us.

Life Principle 6

Everything has its price. *Charactered* people choose wisely and pay their debts.

Life Principle 7

Trust is imperative to the positive human experience. We are all interdependent on others in varying degrees of dependence and independence.

Life Principle One

PERSONAL TRUTHS MUST BE BLENDED WITH UNIVERSAL TRUTHS IN ORDER FOR US TO ENJOY A BALANCED LIFE-STYLE.

You love to snow ski. I prefer tennis. You relax by reading fiction novels. I relax with music. You prefer living single. I want children in my life. One person works in order to play. Another individual thrives on the work itself. These are all examples of personal truths which simply suggest that all of us prefer to travel different roads in life. We're not right or wrong for choosing different preferences. Being true to ourselves often means valuing ourselves enough to pursue the lifestyle of our choice. Personal truths are best enhanced by setting realistic personal goals. Personal truths are directly connected to our personal preferences. They are not necessarily linked to humanity in general.

In order to build our character we decide on many personal truths and commit time and energy to developing them. *Personal Truths* range from wanting better communication in our family to taking a step up the career ladder. Only we know what is true for us. We must constantly revise some of these truths in order to stay current with our changing life situations. We may want to make a list of at least ten personal truths we want to pursue in our lives. We should pay particular attention to our specific needs and values when we design our lists. This list is most effective when it focuses on our "wants," rather than our "musts" and "shoulds."

All of us want to feel loved and to be valued by others. We appreciate our lives more when they include a sincere element of purpose. Friendship is a mutual experience for two sacrificing individuals who willingly prioritize their relationship. These statements are reflective of the numerous feelings and realities that are *universally true*.

The charactered person seeks a healthy blend between his/her personal values and those values of the universe. An individual may love his/her free time but forego some moments of solitude in order to comfort a sick friend. Another person who values peaceful relationships may confront a situation because of integrity. Life is a series of dilemmas and choices. Maintaining a proper perspective about our life is motivating and thus productive. Balancing daily commitments of both a personal and universal nature remains the most challenging and creative high wire act any of us attempt throughout life.

We should seek the answers to our balancing act from within ourselves and from others. Truth is found through both avenues. We are advised to listen to our internal intuitive senses. We also benefit by listening to sound suggestions from others who may have greater life experience than we do. Setting up positive support systems of family and friends and keeping ourselves emotionally healthy so that we are receptive to intuition are the essential tools for successfully walking this balancing high wire in life.

Life Principle Two

CHARACTERED PEOPLE TAKE RESPONSIBILITY FOR THEIR OWN ATTITUDES AND BEHAVIORS.

Character building requires *taking* responsibility for our attitudes and behaviors. The emphasis for *charactered* people is in the action word "take!" They take responsibility while others passively "accept" or even "deny" personal accountability. Immature people often say, "I'm just that way. I've always been that way and I will always stay that way." *With the colored personality labels, we must be cautious that we never use them as a personal excuse, as a judgment of others or a limiting trap for anyone.*

If we hope to be *charactered,* we must be able to present ourselves as a given personality (style) but simultaneously accept responsibility for healthy attitudes and behaviors which may be unnatural to our given personality. For example, we may be a Yellow *personality.* We present ourselves as fun, full of optimism and playful. However, as a *charactered* Yellow we recognize our tendency to be irresponsible. We pay equal attention to our innate fun-loving nature, our optimism, our playful personality, *and* our irresponsible nature. Likewise, a spontaneous, friendly Yellow who also commits willingly to an intimate relationship with sensitivity and honesty is a wonderful blend of a healthy *innate personality* and *developed character.*

Charactered people don't limit themselves or others by personality color labels. They simply use the labels as a way of understanding and accepting basic differences and similarities in all of us. They use these insights as avenues to building rather than blocking human relationships.

Life Principle Three

WE MUST STRETCH AND RISK PERSONAL DISCOMFORT IN ORDER TO MAKE UNNATURAL ATTITUDES AND BEHAVIORS BECOME NATURAL.

Some individuals say they are unable to identify their innate personality from the available options. One individual was confused as to whether his personality was innately Red or Blue. We briefly discussed his dilemma. Suddenly, he said, "I have always been a strong, dominant man. My wife has been dead for several years. I'm just beginning to realize how she influenced my life. My wife was an invalid for most of our married life. Twenty years before she died, she had a serious stroke which limited her physically and forced me to shoulder much of the burden usually shared by a couple. She had been so good to me that I initially felt obligated (and admittedly frustrated) to take care of her. Through the years, however, my feelings of obligations turned to devotion and I genuinely cared for this special woman. Her handicap allowed me to stretch. Eventually, I actually learned how to love."

This *charactered* man is innately a Red personality. He exemplifies many of the strengths we admire in Reds. However, he moved beyond his innate Red limitations and replaced them with positive Blue attributes affording him the enviable combination of Red and Blue strengths. *Charactered* individuals either rise to the tasks placed before them or honestly acknowledge their inadequacies. This man rose to his task with success. *Charactered* people learn to grasp every opportunity (positive or negative) encountered and they give the best that is in them.

Charactered people invite risk into their lives. They want to experience change. Their self-respect is heightened as they face life's discomforts with sincere purpose and clear motives. They do not passively wait for life to test their strength. They seek the opportunities and confront complacency in their daily lifestyle with personal integrity. They are deeply committed to stretching themselves regardless of the inconvenience or discomfort in the character building process of their lives.

Life Principle Four

CHARACTERED PEOPLE LOVE THEMSELVES AND OTHERS.

Recently an article in the newspaper caught my attention. The article mourned the loss of a school crossing guard. She was killed by a car only seconds after pushing seven youngsters to safety. Many remembered her for her unselfish love for children. Risking her life for them is a remarkable statement about her commitment to the children she had loved for so many years. However, she made a far more endearing expression of her love. One child captured the marvelous integrity of this woman who committed her love on a daily basis. The child said, "She'd ask how our classes were going. She was so nice, never grumpy or grouchy."

I asked a group of parents once how many would be willing to die for their children. Each parent raised a hand signifying their devotion to their children. Then I asked how many of them would be willing to commit to loving their children and mates daily with: expressions of love, positive comments, quality time for social activities, reading or games, and by touching them with their hands, their vocal expressions and their eyes! No one raised a hand. "Are you kidding?" one man asked. "I have to earn a living too, you know!" "At least you are honest," I remarked. "But it appears your perception of being a husband and father is somewhat typical. Many of us may be saying we would rather *die* than live for our mates and children!" The crossing guard, remembered by the children, had captured the total picture. In her daily living, she had exemplified her love before she had to die expressing it.

There comes a time in life referred to as the "empty nest" syndrome. (That time in life when the children leave home and some mothers find themselves at a loss for meaning in their lives.) Actually, dads are often left standing out in the cold! Quite often dad missed opportunities to develop their relationship with the children. Mother had expressed her love daily. Dad had been busy earning money to pay the bills.

"I should have seen it coming when they were teenagers," one parent lamented. "That was my first clue that they were more interested in friends and clothes than they were in me. Instead of thinking about some creative options for getting closer, I retreated to my work and television. I think I was scared of them. I didn't understand them. I refused to go to parenting classes. I wouldn't even take up a mutual hobby with my kids. I just expected my wife to handle them. Now they're gone and I can't bring them back." Then he shrugged his shoulder and asked a rhetorical question. "What am I saying, bring them back? How can they come back to a place there they have never been?! I mean they have never 'been' to me and I've never 'been' to them. Not really. We're strangers who shared most everything life offers except ourselves."

Interesting that men (rather than women) express the greatest discomfort with the "empty nest" syndrome. Many men actually break into tears during interviews as they recall the "lost" moments of loving their children. The role of parenting requires a commitment to daily expressions of love, and quality role modeling for children. If this is not done, many face themselves in quiet moments of aging desperation.

We may limit the lives of those we "love" by expecting them to love us the way we are. We limit the character building of those we love when we tell them what they must be and how they should perform because we don't trust them to make the right decisions. Some husbands and wives want to change each other. Some employers hound employees. Some parents overprotect children because they haven't learned to trust themselves nor their children. Rather than granting free agency, we may restrict and monitor the lives of those we feel responsible for. This is not love.

Love is accepting and promoting others. Too many of us think we are wonderful lovers because we "love" others the way *we* would like to be loved. *Love* is always expressed in the "language" of the receiver. Unconditional love is rarely expressed through the eyes of the sender. One woman shared her grief in realizing that all her life she had used people rather than loved them. Now she is aware that all through life she has loved on her terms and simply ignored the needs of others. For example, when she was giving a dinner at her home, she was more concerned about how beautiful the house looked and how delicious the food was than the shared dialogue and friendship her guests would enjoy. She almost cancelled a dinner party one evening because she was so worried about *herself*. Fortunately, just prior to the event we shared a conversation in counseling. We discussed her dilemma and she agreed to pick some things up at the local delicatessen and simply enjoy her guests. The evening was a smashing success and she began to realize how her entire life had been dedicated to the purpose of looking good rather than loving others.

She shared further that she had not given her best friend a Christmas gift the previous year because she couldn't find the perfect gift. Rather than simplifying her efforts of trying to look good and be perfect, she could easily have invited her friend to a special dinner or suggested they meet at a fast food restaurant just to get together. Something personal would have been appreciated by her friend. Unfortunately, she was only concerned with her needs and never realized that being concerned with only *her needs* would never allow her to genuinely say "I love you" to others.

Loving others is most helpful when we accept and promote them as *they* need to be accepted and promoted. It is critical that we recognize the importance of *accepting* each individual as he or she is. Remember, we did not select our personality. It came with us at birth. Each of us is struggling to identify, understand and accept ourself. Perhaps the most valuable gifts we can offer our friends, children and companions, are acceptance, approval and appreciation of their personalities—their unique expression of self, as well as the patience with them in the arduous task of character building.

The element of acceptance immediately brings to light the issue of self-esteem. How well one accepts and appreciates himself has a direct correlation with how well one *can* accept, approve, and/or appreciate others. UNHEALTHY JUDGMENT OF OTHERS COMES FROM OUR OWN PERSONAL INADEQUACY. This is perhaps best illustrated by teenagers. Teenagers are known for their cruelty to peers. Who can't recall being on the hurting end of an unkind comment during those years?

Ask most junior or senior high school students what they value most. The two most commonly stated values are looks and athletic ability. LOOKS AND ATHLETIC ABILITY?! Is there a more gangly, awkward, acne attacked, modulated time in any person's life? No wonder they value what so few of them have at that time of life.

We are most likely to criticize the very thing we crave most. For example, if I am an individual who needs emotional stroking, I am more likely to expect others to provide what I lack than another individual who feels relatively secure and doesn't require excess emotional support. We often criticize others for OUR own inadequacies.

For sometime now we've been told that in order to love others we must first love ourselves. Loving ourselves means we value and accept ourselves as we are, with the understanding that we are endeavoring to improve our shortcomings. It is our self-love that anchors us solidly in healthy loving attitudes and behaviors. When others misunderstand or mistrust our love, we are able to continue loving them because we know our motives are clean. We can genuinely accept that while we may choose to love, others may not yet be prepared to be loved. Loving ourselves frees us of caring for others with any strings attached. When we are too needy, we may be kind and caring for others, but the underlying motives are selfish and potentially controlling of others' behaviors. We may appear to give freely, but there are actually conditions that others must meet in order for us to continue to "love" them.

For example, arrogant people and people who grovel for approval are all suffering from the same need. They are insecure. At times, they may seem to be loving by taking care of others (arrogance) or telling others how they wish they were only as bright or attractive or rich as others (groveling). Arrogance and groveling come from insecurity. Neither are humble. Self-respect produces a humble (teachable) nature which allows us to love unconditionally.

Humility requires that we gain an accurate perspective of ourselves and others. It requires that we value ourselves enough without validation from others. It suggests we are receptive to others' feedback in order to maintain an accurate perception of ourselves and our interpersonal relationships.

Seeking feedback constantly from our children, co-workers, employees and friends regarding our motives is a growth process. Only insecure individuals fear the answers to "How am I doing as a parent, employer or friend?" Secure individuals appreciate truth and opportunities to correct any misunderstandings.

Loving ourselves and others requires candid communication. It is most difficult to find an individual, who, after sharing themselves honestly, has not found a very important place in our heart. We learn to love them. Why? We are endeared to them because they have communicated honestly without *fear* of discovery and rejection. We have experienced the integrity of their human soul. Most of us are grateful to those people who have candidly loved us in our lives. We cherish friends who accepted and approved of our awkward self-discovery; who believed in us and shared that belief without reservation. We value those parents, teachers, friends and children who taught us and nurtured us in the skills of living and the art of loving. We value those who offered us the numerous opportunities that have enabled us to build a strong platform from which we could leap from childhood into adulthood.

With all these experiences we are often simultaneously restless and at peace. We love ourselves, yet we seek enriched life challenges to deepen our ability to love. We have wisdom and yet feel terribly inadequate concerning the mysteries of life. We crave time to share many valuable moments in this human experience with others. We are heartened by meaningful friends that remind us there is always time for those who love us and for those who are willing to be loved.

Life Principle Five

OUR STRENGTHS MUST BE SHARED WITH OTHERS IN ORDER TO FULLY BENEFIT US.

The developing of character begins with desire. The desire is expressed with an action. It may begin as a mental battle, then proceed with an outward search for more knowledge and understanding. Character is not what we have, nor what we do. It is what we are that determines our worth. Character begins with what we think and do when no one else is around, but true character goes beyond personal commitment. *Fully developed character inevitably expresses itself in the giving of service to others.*

Personality can be expressed independently of others. Character must eventually affect the lives of others as well as our own. We may be able to practice in the privacy of our homes, but we cannot fully develop our character alone.

Since all of us are connected in the human condition, do we not share a mutual responsibility to love and accept love from everyone we encounter? How we model love for others often has a significant impact on them and their ability to love others. As we express our love through actions, others watch us and learn from our ways.

We may ask, "Where are our role models? Who are the individuals we most admire?" We find them historically and when we are open and honest, we find them in our current everyday lives.

Florence Nightingale forsook wealth and physical comfort in order to pursue a dream she felt deep within her soul. Knowing men were dying and feeling their pain in her own heart was not enough. She felt driven to hold thousands of men's hands, sharing their emotional devastation and fear while they died one by one, with her at their side. She became the mother of the profession we know and appreciate today as nursing.

Father Damien, the catholic priest who risked everything to serve the lepers on the island of Molokai in Hawaii, fully embraced the principle of sharing for character building. He fought numerous battles with the church bureaucracy to acquire supplies in order to minister to the needs of his "congregation." Eventually he became a leper himself, dying with the people he lived for and loved.

Mahatma Ghandi rendered his entire being to the cause of freedom. His theory of non-violent revolution provided the vehicle which eventually broke the bonds of English subjection for millions of Indians. His greatest statement of character came with one line when he was repeatedly encouraged to write about his life. He resisted for the longest time by simply stating, "My life is my message."

These historical examples of *charactered* role models who shared their strengths for the good of others, may help us identify and appreciate those individuals (including ourselves) in our everyday lives who share themselves for the benefit of all humanity. Recently, some historians seem particularly fond of discrediting public figures by dredging up all their character flaws. I have little doubt that we could find fault with any public role model if we looked hard enough. This merely verifies my contention that character building is no easy task. However, we must realize the wonderful contributions these charactered individuals made to their fellow men, despite their obvious human limitations.

Life Principle Six

EVERYTHING HAS ITS PRICE. CHARACTERED PEOPLE CHOOSE WISELY AND PAY THEIR DEBTS.

The price we pay for reading this book is multifaceted. It may help change aspects of our lives. It may cause pain with the realization that we have been ignoring the development of our character. It costs us time to read when we could be engaging in other activities. It may directly influence our relationships with those we love.

Similarly, there is a price for those who may choose not to read this book. They may miss helpful insights which would enhance their personal and professional lives. They may miss concepts which would open doors for future relationships. One can only imagine the prices we have all paid with our decisions in life. The prices we pay, good or bad, are not ours alone. Everyone connected with us gains or suffers as well.

One individual has been involved in an extra-marital affair for many years without telling his wife. He says he wishes to leave his wife and yet continues to live a double life. His lover explains the prices all three pay. She says, "I can't continue to live like this. We can't go any further with true intimacy because we are living a lie. I want memories of us sharing the holidays with family and friends, but I have to settle for a phone call after his wife goes to sleep." And the man's wife necessarily suffers as well. She experiences the loneliness which comes when one's companion is psychologically withdrawn from a relationship, whether he or she ever acknowledges it or not. Everything has a price. We never pay the price alone.

Our character is much like throwing a pebble in a lake. There is a ripple effect in the water. With greater character, the intensity of our impact increases. We find great reward when we commit to a lifestyle with integrity. A scattered lifestyle offers mixed messages and little intensity because it lacks any real identified purpose. Likewise, we must recognize the high price of a charactered life. It necessarily restricts us from a totally carefree and peaceful existence.

Life Principle Seven

TRUST IS IMPERATIVE TO THE POSITIVE HUMAN EXPERIENCE. WE ARE ALL INTERDEPENDENT ON OTHERS IN VARYING DEGREES OF DEPENDENCE AND INDEPENDENCE.

I have often asked students at the university to guess how many lives touched them prior to our 8:00 a.m. class. The answers usually range from zero to three. That's when the fun begins. The eyes light up and the minds grasp for answers as we consider the clothes they put on (who raised the animals, processed the chemicals, sewed, and retailed their clothing?). Who directly and indirectly furnished their breakfast? Who drove with them or against them in traffic? Who designed, built and repaired their car? Who set the stop lights, paved the roads, and painted road signs? And we've only just begun! Somehow, we typically perceive ourselves as independent agents with little recognition for our interdependence with others. We must always be willing to look at our motives. Taking classes, risking new friendships, seeking therapy, reading books and learning new hobbies can assist us when we have agreed to sincerely see ourselves as we are, and develop a vision of what we hope to become. It is in appreciating our own contributions to humanity and those positive additions others make to our lives that clearly emphasize the value of the life principle known as *interdependence.*

It is not enough to simply choose our *preference* of interest. We commit to a broad spectrum of character development or we suffer the consequences of a limited life. We will find certain areas easy and inviting. Others may require assistance from people we meet throughout our lives. Typically the most common categories of interdependence are Social, Intellectual, Emotional, Financial, Physical, and Spiritual. Spirituality has received an unfortunate rap in its association with organized religion. Spirituality runs far deeper than religion. Spirituality is the light in our eyes, reminding the world that we are well-rooted and "at home" with our purpose in life.

The character building process begins within us. We are the ones who allow ourselves to feel guilty, arrogant, uncommitted or withdrawn. We are responsible for choosing the friends we keep and accepting the lifestyle we live! Uncharactered parents, siblings, teachers and/or other role models may have been examples who taught us limitations rather than strengths. They may have role modeled disappointment rather than creative optimism. Our lives may have crossed with those tragic souls, who, in fearing themselves, taught us to fear our potential. However, all of us can seek and find many other examples of healthy charactered role models. Choosing positive role models is crucial to charactered living. Becoming healthy role models is equally essential to our own personal success.

The power of clean motives and healthy life principles is phenomenal. We can never underestimate the value of clearing our energy sources in order that we become free—free to love, free to change, free to accept ourselves at our worst as well as our best. We can set our goals and commit to a charactered lifestyle which is congruent with those goals. As highly charactered people, we have clean motives. We examine our reasons for behaving or thinking in a particular way. We accept and promote the best in everyone we encounter. We are emotionally and spiritually alive. We are mentally alert and physically disciplined. We honor our commitments.

Examples of *charactered* individuals are: the parent who promotes opportunities and independence but accepts and approves of each child's lifestyle preference; a busy parent who freely gives vacation and/or play time to children; a student who risks a lower grade point average in order to try a more difficult course; a lawyer who defends a client he or she believes in regardless of fee or notoriety; a corporate president who fosters excellence in his or her product and remains equally concerned about employee morale; a teacher who seeks alternative learning modalities in order to reach struggling students.

We can broaden our vision. We can sacrifice life's trivial distractions in order to remain focused on our true purpose in life. WHEN SOUGHT WITH CLEAN MOTIVES, WE CAN BALANCE OUR LIVES BY DEVELOPING ALL STRENGTHS EXPRESSED UNIQUELY BY EACH PERSONALITY. We can exchange our limitations for strengths and enrich our own lives as well as the lives of others we touch. It is an interesting irony that often highly *charactered* individual's personalities are difficult to decipher because they have so artistically and skillfully blended the strengths of others with their own innate strengths. In other words, when our character and personality are blended, our innate personality is no longer always easily recognized.

Character is balance. The three major aspects requiring balance in our individual lives and relationships are (1) passion, (2) personality, and (3) character.

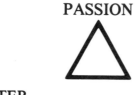

PASSION

CHARACTER   PERSONALITY

PASSION expresses our chemistry. It comes from deep within our subconscious mind. We may feel passionate towards ourselves, another person, or toward a particular hobby or course of study. Passion reflects an unusually strong bonding of emotion. It feels clean and unencumbered. It just feels right and good. This explains why some people are so hard to let go of in relationships, whether they are "best" for us or not. It explains why each of us may be attracted to certain hobbies and careers which others do not find particularly inviting or worthwhile.

PERSONALITY is the color (style) of our self-presentation in life. It defines our innate communication style. It reflects our natural lifestyle and preferential attitudes and behavior. Personality is our unique self-expression. It remains our solid core of attitude and behaviors which gives us our unique identity. We often use our personality as a basis for decisions and connections to various relationships and careers throughout our lives.

CHARACTER represents the responsible attitudes and behaviors we select for our lives. Healthy character is always rooted in truth. It is continually developed throughout our lives by striving to adhere to various Life Principles essential to successful lives, regardless of our culture's influence.

As we balance these three components of relationships, we will feel the confidence which comes from expressing committed, quality lives.

Truth lies within all of us. Nothing and no one can release truth within us without our consent. Even if we are arrogant, critical, devious, or uncommitted, we can ultimately seek, hear and accept that truth. (Our innate personality, or style, is not undesirable. The unique qualities exemplified by each personality offer us opportunities to mix and blend with each other. There are many variations in successful living. It is quite natural for a person to continue developing his or her life with unique preferences.) We must learn to recognize our true motives and commit to healthy Life Principles. In our quest for truth and character, we feel the ultimate joy known only to those individuals who are willing to both risk pain and accept happiness. The most passionate lifestyle is experienced as we artistically weave congruent lifestyles built on both a *positive personality* and a *developed character.*

CHAPTER NINE

The Rainbow Connection: Building Successful Relationships

We understand that Reds enjoy power. We accept the sincerity of the Blues, the gentle touch of the Whites and the charisma of the Yellows. However, we have yet to discuss how daring Reds interact with reluctant Whites. We have no idea how committed Blues and carefree Yellows work together. In order to understand this phenomenon we must investigate the world of relationships.

We established that each color represents natural strengths and limitations. These chapters will review the desirable and undesirable traits which come from the various color combinations. Possible combinations include: Red-Red, Red-Blue, Red-White, Red-Yellow, Blue-Blue, Blue-White, Blue-Yellow, White-White, White-Yellow, and Yellow-Yellow. Each combination offers a unique blend. For example, two Red individuals interact with one another differently than do a Blue and Red couple. A business comprised mostly of Yellows and Whites will operate differently than a business comprised of Yellows and Blues.

Heavy-Weight Versus Light-Weight Personalities

There are general similarities and differences which we should acknowledge prior to focusing on specific combinations. For example, Reds and Blues are the "heavy-weight" personalities, while Whites and Yellows reflect the "light-weights." Similarly there are "the hunters and the hunted" in nature. The lion pursues the antelope. The wolf pursues the lamb. There is an offense and defense in sports. The tackle pursues the quarterback in football. In tennis, the person at the net attacks the person at the baseline. In business, the sales representative pursues the customer.

In life, with these given personalities, the Reds and Blues assume the roles of lion and wolf. They are the football tackles and tennis players who charge the net. They are the sales representative. The Whites and Yellows are the antelope and lamb. They are the football quarterbacks and tennis baseliners. They represent the customers and the consumers. Each role provides an invaluable balance in nature. We could not be as successful without both types of players. Each requires the other. Both have strengths and limitations which enable them to survive as well as contribute. OPPOSITES DO, IN FACT,

ATTRACT EACH OTHER. They enhance each other's lifestyle significantly. Each would be lost without the other. They give credibility to each other. Each serves as a role model to the others for specific areas of character building. Each color gives balance in the full spectrum of relationships.

Intimacy

Blues and Yellows are intimacy-oriented. Blues and Yellows are motivated by intimacy and prefer an emotional connection in securing a strong bonding with others in life. Celebrating romantic occasions, holding hands for no apparent reason and remembering early days of intimacy between a couple are most common for Blues and Yellows. Both colors want to be told often of their romantic allure. In business, they appreciate being noticed and often determine whether to stay in a particular job based on the shared intimacy at work.

Blues and Yellows understand their needs for intimacy at a much more subconscious level than they realize. For example, one major reason Yellows are so demonstrative is their inner desire to be touched. Many Yellows never understand why they are so physical but, in truth, they may be simply reaching out for what they need.

Power

Reds and Whites are power-based. Reds and Whites expend a lot of energy toward preserving the balance of power in the relationship and other practical issues. One White woman demanded that her Red husband repay her the money he had borrowed following a therapy session. I suggested that her timing was not the best for the relationship. She said, rather blandly, that it needed to be done since it was already overdue, and besides, she was trying to learn how to be assertive. Actually, she was striving to balance the power.

Reds and Whites want the conveniences of companionship without all the complex emotional strings attached. Subconsciously, they understand each other's style and often position themselves in the most strategic situations in order to maintain control of their relationships. Reds are far more direct in their pursuit of power than Whites. Whites often use a "passive-aggressive" approach to their power orientation. (Passive-aggressive refers to accepting certain behaviors without negative reactions and then aggressively getting even in a relationship at a later date through a totally different set of circumstances.)

An example of passive-aggressive is the mother who tells her son that he can go outside and play football, *but* can't get his clothes dirty. When the son comes home filthy, she gladly tosses the clothes in the washer but neglects to fix his dinner until much later than usual that evening. She is terribly upset by his behavior, but rather than confront him at the time, she *gets even* later in an unrelated incident.

Communication Style

Another unique style differentiation lies in communication. Reds and Yellows are more inclined to tell people things to do while Blues and Whites are more likely to ask people for their opinions. Whites and Blues are comfortable in seeking advice on certain dilemmas while Reds and Yellows prefer to give the solutions. Reds and Yellows tend to blame others. Blues and Whites blame themselves. Reds respond best to direct, logical communication. (Whatever you do, don't cry!) Blues prefer a softer, emotional style of feedback. They tend to be hardest on themselves with their perfectionistic tendency. Negative feedback is most effective for Blues when offered empathetically. Whites cannot be yelled at. They prefer a gentle honesty with low conflict profile. Yellows enjoy a casual (even humorous) style in receiving feedback. They appreciate warmth and reassurance.

Self-Esteem

All colors seek self-satisfaction and self-esteem with a unique flare. Self-esteem has become a particularly interesting component of personality in this century. Parents want to know how self-esteem and productivity are connected. Teachers want to understand how learning and self-esteem interact. One of the most significant findings in the color theory is the difference in how each personality reflects self-esteem.

Reds and Yellows appear to have higher self-esteem than Blues and Whites at birth. Blue and White children tend to have self-defeating attitudes. They criticize themselves and feel inadequate. Most Red and Yellow children tend to project themselves, criticize others and openly display more positive self-regard. All personalities, however, come with some positive self-regard and some negative feelings of insecurity.

Reds appear most self-assured of all the colors, and yet, they tend to be the most insecure. They are not originally less secure, but because they disguise their insecurity they often delay character development which can only come by exposing themselves emotionally (being vulnerable) and taking responsibility for their insecurities. Unfortunately, Reds hide their insecurities so well that few people recognize their need to grow up emotionally. They are often allowed to slide emotionally because they are so stubborn. Most people are typically unwilling to invest the necessary energy to deal with them. Reds willingly dive from the highest diving board and scale the most difficult mountain in order to maintain their competent and secure image.

Yellows often manage to maintain a superficial social snobbery, thus protecting themselves from real intimate exposure of their insecurity. Whites and Blues are far less likely to exert the energy necessary to overtly hide their insecurities.

Consequently, when we look at self-esteem, we consistently come up with the supposition that Reds and Yellows appear stronger than the Blues and Whites. Perhaps the Reds and Yellows maintain strong self-images because society (especially parents and teachers) perceive the initial behavior of Reds and Yellows as strong and treat them with this perception. As a result, Reds and Yellows theoretically develop even greater self-regard. The Blues and Whites openly reveal their insecurities and society often responds with a protective, coddling or condescending manner. This encourages a potential lifetime pattern of self-degradation and/or martyrdom.

Unfortunately, Reds and Yellows often fall prey to a "self satisfaction syndrome." Perhaps they feel so good about themselves that they simply slide through life rather than extending the effort to earn a deeper self-respect. This self-respect only comes from confronting personal inadequacies and choosing to contribute to others. On the other hand, Blues and Whites may develop deeper self-esteem later in life because they recognize and acknowledge their deficiencies and put forth the necessary effort to feel better about themselves. Unfortunately, some may feel overwhelmed by their feelings of inadequacy and live out their entire life with fear and guilt complexes.

All personalities find true self-esteem only after honest self-analyzation and loving commitment to promoting the well-being of themselves and others. Self-esteem is gained slowly and often painfully by risking exposure to others. Many individuals are willing to have shallow relationships in order to avoid disclosing negative personality traits and/or character flaws. Charactered people value self-esteem enough to pay the price of continued risk throughout various phases of life.

Involvement Versus Isolation

Reds and Yellows are alert and focus directly on practicalities and task. (Remember, for Yellows, task often means play.) Blues and Whites tend to think in terms of the past and the future, while Reds and Yellows concern themselves predominantly with the present. Blues and Whites are the daydreamers and are often preoccupied in life.

We need to afford Reds and Yellows their task-orientation. Blues and Whites deserve time for creativity or quiet reflection. We enhance relationships when we promote opportunities for individuals within the relationship to pursue their style of life. Demanding that a Yellow reflect quietly for too long may be more destructive than productive if the individual isn't prepared for such an experience.

Educators (typically Blue) can be most counter-productive to Red students if they refuse to afford them task leadership opportunities. Most Blues will feel frustrated if they are restricted in their time to meditate and plan prior to taking action or making a decision. Whites typically become silently stubborn when they are ordered to move faster or become too aggressive on a project. Each color responds most effectively to given situations when allowed, within reason, to follow their preferred style.

Therapeutic Intervention Style

Every psychotherapist has the opportunity of serving in the role of a "change-agent." In order to be effective, the approach should be altered to match the specific needs of the patients. There is a high correlation between the patient's personality and the style of intervention. Reds and Blues are far more resistant to change, while Yellows and Whites are initially more receptive to the change process. Resistance comes in a less direct and abrasive manner for the

Blues than the Reds. The intensity of the resistance is, however, fairly equal. On the other hand, Yellows are more verbally receptive to change than the Whites. However, both generally appear receptive and willing to adapt their lifestyles.

Just the reverse is true of these personalities in terms of follow-through and completion of the change process. Reds and Blues are far more likely to successfully commit themselves to the changing process once their resistance is removed. Yellows and Whites are more inclined to slip back into old behavior patterns or feel unmotivated to complete the change process.

Therapeutically, Blues and Reds demand answers. They want specific methods, solutions and direction once they decide to change. They request behavioral therapy which focuses on specific homework assignments and expectations. The most frustrating aspect of therapy for them is coming to the realization that the therapist will not and cannot necessarily design a specific behavioral process with long term success for them. What they actually need most is an attitudinal adjustment.

Attitudinal therapy forces them to examine their motives and clear up unhealthy perceptions. Reds suffer most often from inaccurate emotional messages such as hidden insecurities, blocking communication or layers and years of denied anger. Blues suffer most often from irrational thinking. They have usually relied so heavily on their "emotional muscles" that their ability to think rationally is seriously impaired. This process of attitudinal readjustment takes much longer and requires more patience than the behavioral process. Subsequently, Reds and Blues often become frustrated with psychotherapy.

Quite differently than with Reds and Blues, the approach with the Whites and Yellows is more direct and behavioral. It is the kind of therapy Reds and Blues would really prefer. Generally, Yellows and Whites have positive and receptive attitudes, but their discipline and motivation often leaves a lot to be desired. They require constant support with new techniques for effectively tackling life. Particularly challenging is working with a couple requiring different approaches (i.e.,, a Yellow-Red couple). The Red often complains that the therapist attacks him or her too much in the session. The Yellow complains that he or she has more homework than the Red after the session is over.

Yellows and Whites need to see themselves completing goals and disciplining themselves consistently over a long period of time in order to increase their self-esteem and develop healthy lifestyles. Giving a Red or Blue more hobbies or tasks will do little to increase self-esteem since they are already driven to achieve and produce and probably don't feel that what they do is good enough. They need to increase their awareness of self-flagellating (Blue), or arrogant (Red) feelings and thoughts in order to be more accepting of themselves and others.

Reds and Blues want immediate action and behavior modification. They most often get a time consuming, attitudinal adjustment and must struggle with it. Yellows and Whites want a relaxed, attitudinal approach. They get a direct process, requiring commitment and behavior modification and they find it taxing to endure. Once they accept a "no pain—no gain" philosophy, they can modify their behavior.

Blues and Whites are more non-verbal while Reds and Yellows generally share strong verbal skills. (In other words, the strong, silent type isn't a Red personality at all. He or she is a White.) Reds and Yellows also tend to think very quickly on their feet, while Blues and Whites spend a lot of time kicking themselves for not having had the best retort at the time of the conversation. They often come up with great lines due to their creative wit. Unfortunately, the thought is two days too late.

It has been suggested that *a life unexamined is hardly a life worth living.* Knowing ourselves brings a rich depth that makes our journey through life much more meaningful for ourselves and others. It also enhances our opportunities to change those limitations which deter our ability to contribute. It enhances our opportunities to develop the strengths which define our uniqueness in how and what we contribute. Hopefully, you will be receptive to learning about yourself and understanding those around you as we look at specific color combinations.

IT IS IMPORTANT TO UNDERSTAND THE CHARACTERISTICS OF *ALL* THE PERSONALITIES IN ORDER TO APPRECIATE HOW WE AND OTHERS SEE THE WORLD. No element of nature operates well in a vacuum. Each personality relies on the others to fully experience its true color. Learn about the personalities without judgment. Seek to appreciate the unique strengths and limitations in others. Strengthen your inherent limitations in order to get along better with others. Limitations can become strengths. Strive to recognize the natural bonding or resistance that various personalities experience. In accordance with the prayer of St. Francis of Assisi, "Grant that (we) may not so much seek to be understood as to understand."

The following chart illustrates the similarities and differences among the personalities in the total color spectrum.

Personality Connections

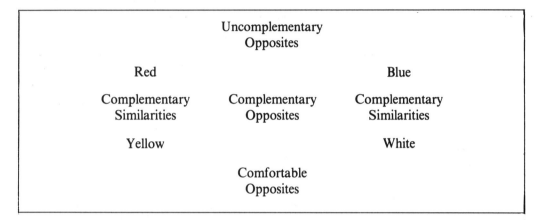

Personality Connections Graph

Let me explain this graph. By definition, *complementary* suggests "an adding to the effect of" or "supplying what is lacking." By the literal definition, then, each color complements every other color with their innate strengths. However, this chart presents a looser definition in order to help us understand the realities of color combinations rather than simple theory.

Some colors are more similar than others. Reds and Yellows share a natural likeness. They share similar styles in their strong verbal skills, insensitivity, and positive action orientation. Blues and Whites are similar in their non-verbal preference, sensitivity, and desire to accomodate others. When a person's personlity is a combination of Red-Yellow or Blue-White, they find the blend very comfortable and cooperative within themselves.

Some colors are uniquely opposite but appeal to each other for a sense of completion and to make them feel whole. Reds and Whites enjoy a practical orientation to relationships and rely on facts and common sense to light their way. They share similar perceptions of power, excitement and leadership. Blues and Yellows mutually seek intimacy, romance, and fantasy. Both sets of colors offer a natural balance within themselves. Subsequently, Reds-Whites and Blues-Yellows are most inclined to find themselves in committed relationships with each other. However, when *one* individual experiences either of these blends within himself/herself, he/she finds a perpetual split in focus and must commit to the dominant motive in order to find harmony within his/her attitudes and behavior.

Some colors do not find their blending to feel naturally complementary and/or innately comfortable. Red-Blue and White-Yellow combinations find themselves in this category. Reds and Blues generally experience the greatest conflict because (1) they are such strong personalities, and (2) their innate motives of power and intimacy provide an awkward blend. People with a Red-Blue personality, experience the same awkwardness within themselves as two individuals with Red and Blue personalities feel in their relationship. They must work harder on their character in order to facilitate the potential strength of this innate uncomplementary connection.

White-Yellow combinations do not offer each other completion. They are both easy going and unlikely to commit in business or marriage because without a lot of character development, both lack the necessary strength to be successful in a shared committed relationship. As uncomfortable as Red-Blue combinations are, they are far more likely to connect than Whites and Yellows. However, an individual with the White-Yellow blend enjoys strong people skills and rarely feels much inner conflict due to the innate gentleness of each personality.

The film classic, *Gone with the Wind,* offers us a vivid presentation of the colors in relationships. The leading characters represent the different personalities and provides us with a visual portrayal of how the colors interact.

Scarlett O'Hara was a Red. Influenced by power and a strong will to be right, she brilliantly orchestrated her survival despite the overwhelming turmoil of the Civil War. Her great love was Rhett Bulter, whose charismatic and flamboyant lifestyle illustrated the Yellow personality. His attraction to Scarlett was eventually doomed because of the intimacy he craved and she would never give.

Ashley embodies the loyalty and high moral standards of the Blue. He consistently rebuked Scarlett's romantic overtures despite his attraction to her because he sensed her emotional insecurities and inadequacy to meet his needs for genuine intimacy. Melanie, on the other hand, offered peace and support to all three characters. She represented the White. She never suspected Ashley or Scarlett of anything less than moral and proper behavior. She defended Scarlett to her enemies. She warmly received Rhett into the family. She loved Ashley to her dying breath. Interestingly, Rhett and Ashley (Yellow and Blue) were quite compatible despite their different backgrounds.

Each character embodies the essence of personalities within relationships. Uniquely, their color defined their preferences, limitations and motivations better than any writer could illustrate. Their relationships were instinctively decided before they ever met on the Southern Plantation of Tara.

In this spirit of understanding, let's look at the specific relationships. The following comparisons offer a quick glance at how the different personalities interact in their most raw and natural form. With a developed character, you may find that some of the statements do not completely reflect your current style. Simply make a note of how your character development has replaced innate personality limitations and added new dimensions to your life. With rare exception, the *motives,* the *needs* and the *wants* remain accurately in place. The most important concept here is to identify how you (and those you care about) are *motivated* and what style you should choose to use while interacting with others.

Now it's your opportunity to see yourself and how your relationships connect. Review the motives, needs, wants and behaviors and determine your own compatibility.

Rainbow

Look for the various combinations you encounter in your life. Ask yourself why you seek the combinations you do. Consider how the color combinations of your parents and yourself impacted your life. Reflect on the relationship between your employers (or employees) and yourself. Seek to understand how your personality influences and is influenced by others. How do the different combinations impact you? Which combination do you find most intimidating and why? Which combination feels most comfortable to you? Why do you listen to certain colors more than others? Why is a clean home so important to one individual and relatively meaningless to another? Does a "yeller and screamer" really mean the awful things she or he says? How do we accept or redirect laziness in others? Why do I link up with people who spend money lavishly, while I save everything I earn?

Consider the wonderful possibilities you can use these insights for in your life. Whether you are selecting a candidate for a job, a friend or trying to make sense out of a parent-child relationship, the rainbow connection is invaluable. Determining the depth of one's character is important in understanding people as unique individuals rather than groupies of a particular color. However, we can rest assured that everyone operates best within their own innate personality. Therefore, despite the obvious limitations each color has, we can generally trust that we will behave, at least to some degree, in similar manner to our defined personality color group.

Each personality combination brings with it a unique set of strengths and limitations. With developed character and an understanding of innate personalities, we are able to deal with the specific needs of each possible combination, whether it be in the role of friend, lover, parent, employer, or child. Learning to facilitate relationships without jeopardizing our integrity is essential to our success in life.

CHAPTER TEN

The Red Connections

Fireworks

RED-RED RELATIONSHIPS

Red-Red relationships are typically the most dynamic of all the color connections. Both people are direct, decisive and determined. They are such intense people that everything about their relationship is generally bold interaction and high profile.

One close friend told me about her childhood with two very Red parents. Her father came home one evening from working in the fields and became so angry when dinner wasn't ready that he took the uncooked beans from the stove and threw them out in the back yard. This infuriated his wife who quickly responded by taking his rifle from the kitchen and tossing it out by the beans. Each one in turn, kept tossing things from the kitchen until it was almost empty and their backyard a cluttered mess. Then they both looked at each other, laughed and went out to eat at a restaurant, leaving their children to fend for themselves.

RED RULES OF LIFE

(and there are only two)

Rule 1: Reds are *ALWAYS* right.
Rule 2: If (and that's a huge if) Reds are wrong, see Rule 1.

This powerful combination can be highly productive. They are task-oriented and find little need for concentrating on intimacy or compassion towards each other. Both typically enjoy the leadership role and since there is usually only room for one "king of the jungle," they tend not to attract each other for long term commitments. Reds are more likely to seek companions with a softer, more compassionate side.

Healthy Red relationships often exist and flourish within a friendship, career or even parent-child relationship. However, Red-Red combinations are not generally well represented in marital relationships.

Mutual respect is the key element of a Red-Red relationship. They must learn to respect each other because of their intense strength. Respect affords Reds the opportunity of accepting each other's point of view. When they value each other's perspective, they are more likely to alter some of their decisions in order to share mutual dreams. Otherwise Red-Red relationships merely reflect two separate people living their own life with little evidence of a shared lifestyle.

When Reds refuse to share decision making and accept each other's perceptions, they suffer an intolerable stalemate in their relationship. How do two people get anywhere when both of them are absolutely certain that they know the best way to get there and neither can agree? This dilemma is not uncommon with two Reds in any given relationship. Most Red children are certain that *they* know a better way to raise children than their parents. They "are" right and nothing the parent can say or do seems to convince them otherwise. Most Red parents are certain that *they* know the only way to raise children and nothing the child can say or do seems to convince them otherwise.

Reds demand the right to control their own lives as well as the lives of anyone who will allow it (including other Reds). Since both Reds in any relationship want control, it often becomes a matter of who has the greater power. Typically Red parents have greater control over their Red children, and Red employers have the edge over Red employees. I was raised in a large family with a very powerful Red mother who clearly dominated our lives. In developing the color theory, I was initially stumped in assessing the personalities of my own brothers and sisters. My mother was so powerful that we *all* acquiesced to her superiority. (In our later years, we nicknamed her the "Little General" reflecting her dominant manner.) As children, no one crossed her (and lived to talk about it)! Her dominance so far exceeded the natural power of her children that I neglected initially to see any Red personalities among my brothers and sisters. They were dominated by a more powerful Red and unable to accurately reflect their innate personalities until they left home and developed families of their own. Crossing a Red in their own territory is like trying to tell a New York taxi cab driver that he doesn't know how to drive. Good Luck!!

Despite the typical dominance of Red parents, society is replete with numerous examples of Red children asserting themselves with their parents. Relatively few of the Red youth I have known have survived the teenage years without vowing to leave home before they were eighteen. One Red sixteen year old client, Linda, was in direct conflict almost daily with her Red stepfather, Rick. She struggled to comply with his "unreasonable" curfews and numerous parental expectations in order to accommodate her White mother. Accepting her dad's rules seemed impossible. Earning her own way in the world seemed far more appealing than continually subjecting herself to her dad's control. She resisted any authority or control. She resented school, so she refused to study. She detested "waiting in limbo" to grow up.

One day I asked her, "Linda, since you are so unhappy, have you ever thought of leaving home and moving out on your own?!" Her eyes seemed to pierce mine with the dullest and yet most defiant stare. Coldly, and convincingly, she said, "I have contemplated that a thousand times." By her tone of voice, I knew she wasn't exaggerating.

She ran away from home two weeks later. She preferred to sleep on a couch at a friend's, work for minimum wage and put up with an employer's demands, than prolong what seemed like "lifetime servitude" to her Red stepfather.

Note: She returned home within a month with a greater appreciation for her parents. However, she still struggles with parental leadership and authority.

Reds do not like or value anyone who dictates their destiny. Yet, they are quite comfortable dictating the destiny of others. (Of course, they are. If you had all the answers, wouldn't you feel compelled to design and dictate other's futures for them?!") The price for this power-orientation and lack of mutual respect is high. Intimacy rarely flourishes with the constant battle cries of debate. Positive energy is often deferred in order to provide ample opportunity to defend one's position. Sharing feelings becomes a secondary consideration because vulnerability is seen as non-productive in a defensive and combative atmosphere. When two Reds are certain that they are right, and refuse to respect each other, the result can be similar to the pounding of a jack hammer against cement.

HIGHLY MOTIVATED

Most relationships involving a Red, revolve around the Red personality. Reds are so bold and dominant. When they feel strongly about having a family reunion, a family reunion is held whether others plan to attend or not. Two healthy Reds make an unflappable duo. They carry their own motivation within themselves. They push each other with strong expectations and become a highly organized front.

One Red parent and Red child were so motivated to work out their differences that they set a record in my office for short term therapy. Selfish as Reds tend to be, these two patients had one goal—to escape my office. I never saw two individuals learn diplomacy and acceptance more rapidly than this pair. Their motivation actually promoted good relations within the home until genuine attitudinal changes could follow and further insure positive parent-child relations.

LACK OF EMOTIONAL GARBAGE

Reds are greatly benefitted by the limited emotional garbage they allow in their lives. Reds don't require many emotional support systems in order for them to perform well. Subsequently they are thrilled to share a task because neither needs to remember to acknowledge the other Red with "warm fuzzies" and/or repeated statements of appreciation. "Just get it done and forget the feelings!" they shout.

A highly successful Jewish businessman conducted a major business transaction with an individual in Germany. Both were very Red and highly competent in their fields. Upon entering the German's office, the Jewish businessman was stunned to see Facist signs and pictures depicting this man's obvious sympathy for Nazi Germany. World War II had only recently ended and the fresh memories of the Nazi's brutal extermination of thousands of Jews brought a terrible anger within my patient. He was actually sickened to be with this individual whom he instantly hated. However, business was business, and his purpose in being there was to conduct a business meeting. He pulled himself together and successfully completed their transaction, forgetting the flag and other memorabilia which initially brought him tremendous personal trauma. Despite his continued anger, he successfully maintained a productive business relationship with this man.

Reds are rarely discouraged. They don't typically drain each other with emotional blackmail (i.e., "Either you spend time with me or I won't go to your mother's house for dinner."). They are generally independent and enjoy their self-sufficient natures. They don't spend a lot of energy trying to make each other feel loved. They are more concerned with productivity and accomplishment.

SHARED VALUES OF PRODUCTIVITY

Reds often push each other to be productive. They enjoy the shared trust they have in knowing each other is highly responsible and will "come through" with whatever assignments they have agreed to complete. Reds enjoy a shared value of time. They are fast paced and determined. Subsequently, they enjoy working together and experiencing many accomplishments due to their strong task-orientation.

One Red author was writing a book with a Blue friend. His Blue friend belabored every point to perfection. The Red author was furious each week with his friend's lack of productivity. He completed all his sections of the book only to be held up by his Blue friend who was unable to simply produce. "I only regret not writing it by myself or with another Red," he said. He readily agreed that his Blue friend's writing was brilliant but feared the perpetual delay of getting the book published if his friend didn't cut the perfection stuff and simply produce. Reds appreciate productivity and are more likely to respect those who share similar beliefs.

PRODUCTIVE GOAL SETTING

One Red married couple was terribly successful in accomplishing goals. They were proud that they both loved goal setting and willingly gave it high priority in their relationship. The woman commented, "We go to Las Vegas or some fun place alone every six months and evaluate our successes and failures. Then we establish a new set of goals for the next six months. I can't tell you how exciting it is to lay in bed with your spouse and feel more challenged than you do with your business colleagues. I often feel like we are cooperatively competing with each other to see who can most creatively produce the most exciting and successful life."

EXTREME COMPETITION

While cooperative competition is highly productive, Red-Red relationships are equally susceptible to extreme competition, which produces negative interaction. This color combination probably travels further and accomplishes more than most relationships. The question is the quality (rather than quantity) of their trips. Red-Red relationships most probably will arrive first at the top of the mountain. (They are highly task-oriented and value completion of any activity.) However, while they are at the top of the mountain, the others may well be further down the path enjoying a wild flower or exquisite sunset the Reds missed in their hurry to complete the hike. Reds often arrive at life's end with few moments that really capture their hearts. More often their walls are lined with numerous trophies and conquests. They remind me of the couple that travels in Europe in order to come home and tell everyone where they went. The "going" appears to be less appealing than the "having been". They often live in the future with a sense of triumph for having completed a determined goal. Many Red parents comment on how pleased they are with how well their children "turned out," while other personalities reminisce about moments they shared as a family in the growing years. Red-Red relationships often miss the pure enjoyment of the activity they are mutually engaged in or, perhaps they simply enjoy it differently than other personalities do.

Due to their competitive natures, Red-Red relationships seem to be more prone to obsessive-compulsive behavior than other personality combinations. One Red married couple reflects the common trend in the working world for Reds. They have put off having children for ten years in order to build a successful business. Their entire world revolves around the business world. Their social engagements are always connected with helping the business. Evenings spent alone generally focus on business-related conversation. Reading material is typically work-oriented. They are financially secure and yet have great difficulty finding the "stop button" or "shift focus button" because of their obsession with the business.

Overeating and dieting are common obsessions with Red couples, as well. Community or church work are noted commitments Reds make in life. They can become compulsive about completing tasks or promoting causes and hardly notice whether other relationship intimacies (or lack thereof) even exist. Whatever the obsession or compulsion, Red-Red relationships are most assuredly productive and proactive. They will surge ahead whether the cause is worthy or not. As long as they feel gratified by the relationship, Reds will bulldoze through any obstacles to meet the needs of the relationship.

Competitive natures can be very healthy, when done in the spirit of cooperation. Maintaining a proper perspective on their competitiveness is difficult for two Reds because they tend to see things in terms of winning or losing with little gray area in between. Red-Red relationships prefer to win and dedicate themselves to that end, but if they must lose, they will often cause others to lose as well.

They are highly competitive and willingly pay whatever price is necessary in order to come out on top of any experience they deem valuable enough to pursue. This style of relationship necessitates a highly communicative interaction. Reds display a remarkable ability and willingness to confront each other. They are equally inclined to express hostility and aggression towards each other, as well.

COMMUNICATION

Red companions tend to be highly critical of each other in a relationship. They are also prone to unite and mock others outside of the relationship in a critical manner. I remember one family with a set of Red twin boys who ridiculed each other mercilessly and yet, they could unite and turn on their parents or other siblings in a flash. They were often negative and dominated most family activities with their critical nature.

Reds generally come to relationships equipped with powerful verbal skills. They are quick with the tongue and can banter with the best of them. When you put two angry Reds together it is similar to two speeding jets crashing in mid-air. No one ever truly wins. It is a loss for both. On numerous occasions, I have had to stand up and wave my hands during a therapy session with two Reds just to pull them off each other's verbal assaults. Some would spend the entire time attacking each other if there wasn't a referee. Neither wants to give the other one the satisfaction of "winning" so they keep at the same issues long after the issues should be laid to rest.

Reds do not usually listen well. Typically, Reds are very impatient listeners. When they do hear, they selectively hear only those parts of the conversation which they agree with or accept. If Reds are not careful, they will set themselves up for living separate, rigid lives because they are unwilling to accept what each other has to say. Reds are often poor listeners because they need to be right. They refuse to hear what others say if they perceive that it may force them to accept and admit their own mistakes or limitations and change their behavior.

This unwillingness to listen is illuminated in the following example of a Red married couple. One night they were playing around and he began biting her (nibbling at first and more painful later on). For five years she had repeatedly asked him to stop biting her. He refused to listen and repeatedly suggested that it was fun and playful. He never really believed she was serious.

This night he was biting her and it really hurt. She told him to stop and he simply laughed it off, ignoring her requests. She became so angry that she finally carried through on a threat she had been making for years and popped him in the mouth as hard as she could. He couldn't believe it. She couldn't either, but now there was no turning back for either of them. Both went after each other physically until their three children were frantic with fear. Imagine the scene. The young children unitedly tried to pull each parent from the other. The husband yanked the phone from the wall so no one could call for help and continued to assault his wife and kids. Finally his wife forced him out of the house and locked the doors. He spent the night in his car and would hardly speak the next day when she finally let him back in the house.

For years, she had demanded that he stop biting her. For years, he had refused to hear. When we discussed it in my office the following day he could not see how his inability to listen had played a major role in the conflict. If he had simply heard her requests for not biting, which had been made over a five year period, this incident would never have taken place. Unfortunately, he could only see how *she* had overreacted ("I didn't bite her *that* hard") and unfairly locked him out of his own house. Reds find it difficult to listen without trying to win conversations. They are notorious for wanting the last word rather than hearing the last feeling.

Reds can be very insensitive in conversation. They are more concerned with presenting perceived facts than generating kind feelings. I still laugh when I think back to a comment a Red mother made at a family gathering. Picture all five of her adult male children and their spouses seated at a dinner table. Grandchildren were running around outside. A beautiful dinner had been prepared and enthusiastic conversations had ensued. Toward the end of the dinner, the subject of one brother's depression came up. The Red mother boldly stated, "I don't understand what his problem is. I have five boys and they were all perfect when they left my home. I guess it all started in their marriages." The Red daughter-in-laws were furious. The gauntlet had been thrown down and simple discussion would not suffice. Needless to say, a most enjoyable family dinner was quickly, and rather abruptly, ended. Problem resolution and mutual understanding is rarely experienced in Red-Red relationships because the conversations often lack intimacy as reflected by listening and acceptance of responsibility by either person.

One of the most positive aspects of a Red-Red communication is their willingness to confront each other on almost all issues at anytime. No tiptoeing or walking on egg shells is necessary here. Reds have little regard (and less respect) for dishonest diplomacy. If you have something to say in a relationship, Reds feel it should be said. If the other person has a problem with that, Reds feel the other person has the problem. Reds willingly take the initiative in confronting each other directly and thus, enjoy a rare strength in the communication process. I have often known two Reds to end up laughing at themselves following heated arguments which would have silenced other personalities for days. They have a refreshing ability to look at issues rather than always focusing on the personal side of conflict.

LACK OF WARMTH

Warmth is not a word often used to describe Red-Red relationships. They are so intense, critical and tactless that they do not exude or cultivate a lot of gentleness or provide much accommodation in their interpersonal relations. Most Reds have difficulty in sharing positive feelings. Unfortunately, they have little difficulty sharing negative feelings. Of all the personalities, Reds are probably most comfortable with the feeling of anger. They express it often, along with many other critical and negative emotions. However, they are often slow to respond with positive, supportive comments.

ACTIVE

Reds are particularly active people. As a twosome they will generate a lot of energy and involvement. They often find calendaring with each other's schedules essential in order to maintain good communication. Rather than assuming a secondary position of support they both head off in whatever directions feel personally fulfilling which requires a high degree of tolerance and constant feedback. One Red couple lists everything on the chalkboard by the telephone. Unfortunately, when one feels their activity is more important for both to attend than the previously listed activity, they simply cross out the first entry and display their own. Imagine the interesting communication that promotes!!!

Red-Red relationships share so many powerful characteristics (positive and negative) that it behooves all Reds to develop their assets and alter their liabilities. The positive values that many Red-Red relationships share include: mutual respect, high motivation, lack of emotional garbage, high productivity, effective goal-setting, willingness to confront issues and each other, and strong activity orientation. The negative liabilities include: lack of intimacy, power struggles focused on "winning" and "being right," lack of compromise, extreme competition, insensitive communication and lack of warmth.

Blood, Sweat and Tears

RED-BLUE RELATIONSHIPS

No other combination of personalities must work as hard for successful compatibility as Reds and Blues. Both want to be in control. They are equally strong and determined individuals. Unfortunately, this is about all they innately share in common. Their motives, needs, wants and behaviors are mostly opposite. Theirs is a difficult union regardless of the various roles they may play in the relationship.

OVERVIEW

Red Personality	Blue Personality
MOTIVE	
Power	Intimacy
NEEDS	
to be right	to be understood
to be respected	to be appreciated
to look good to others (academically)	to be good for self (morally)
approval	acceptance
WANTS	
challenging adventure	security
leadership	autonomy
to please self	to please others
to hide insecurities (tightly)	to reveal insecurities (openly)
BEHAVIOR STYLE	
highly complex	highly complex
high productivity	strong perfectionism
controlling of others	controlling of self and others

enjoys a high profile	prefers a low profile
welcomes change	prefers stability
logical (unemotional)	emotional (irrational)
insensitive	too sensitive
delegator	doer
manipulative	manipulative
impatient	impatient, but long suffering
direct communication (with facts)	direct communication (with feelings)
innovative	creative
intense	intense
demanding	demanding
unforgiving, but moves on	unforgiving and resentful
confrontive	confrontive
strong verbal	strong non-verbal
possessive	possessive
tactless	tactful
rebellious	behaved
responsible	responsible
achiever	achiever
gives advice and expects compliance	gives advice and expects compliance
does not seek advice	seeks advice from knowledgeable people
intimidating	intimidating
critical of others	critical of self and others
arrogant	self-righteous
gives others guilt	often feels guilty
conflict-oriented if necessary to get own way	willing to deal with conflict for principles
proactive	negative
poor listener	caring listener
difficult to share feeling with	complex and deep when sharing feelings

doesn't love easily, but strong commitment	loves deeply and disappointed by those who can't love (maintains strong commitment)
defiant to law and rules lies to save face	compliant with rules lies to spare others feelings due to embarrassment

INTERPERSONAL RELATIONSHIPS
(In-depth Presentation)

POWER   versus   INTIMACY

   The greatest struggle for Reds and Blues may well be based in their differing motives. Reds are motivated by power and Blues are motivated by intimacy. Neither offers the other what is wanted without first demanding that their needs be met as well. For example, the following conversation reflects their unique perspectives.

Red: "Do what I say and we'll get along just fine."

Blue: "Tell me you love me and I'll walk to the ends of the earth for you."

   Typical frustration between Blues and Reds involve perceptions of intimacy.

   A Blue wife commenting on her Red husband:

"He never really loved me. Twenty-five years ago we went on our honeymoon and ended up staying with his sister who I had never even met. We slept on their living room couch. He would leave me with his sister while he went hunting and fishing with his buddies every day. One day I became physically ill with food poisoning and when he finally came home one night at 11 p.m., all he said was, 'I heard you were sick. Are you better now?' He had a great honeymoon with his buddies and at the time I thought maybe he needed that after all the hoopla with the wedding. I remember being down by the lake one day and watching a couple walking hand in hand. I wept for two hours over it. I've always built my world around him. He has never done the same for me."

One sixty year old Blue woman finally relinquished her struggle for intimacy with her Red husband and became a volunteer for Traveler's Aid at the airport. She realized that he was a wonderful man. She didn't want a divorce, so she redirected her needs for intimacy to other people. It isn't the same as receiving her husband's affection, but it is much healthier than continuing the battle for the intimacy he neither understands or apparently values.

CHALLENGING ADVENTURE   versus   SECURITY

Red: "C'mon, let's live a little. After all, we only go around once. We've made money before and we can do it again. Nothing is going to happen and if it does, we'll figure out a solution. We always have before."

Blue: "I don't feel good about making lots of changes right now. We should wait until things settle down before we try something else. You're so old. You can't start a new business at this late date. What will I do if you die and leave me with all these bills?!"

PLEASES SELF   versus   PLEASES OTHERS

Reds are basically selfish, while Blues enjoy being self-sacrificing. If a family were making banana splits, and there was a limited supply of ice cream, the Red would try to talk one of the others into having something else so he or she would get the banana split. The Blue would find something else to eat and give the full banana split portions to the others.

TO HIDE INSECURITIES   versus   TO REVEAL INSECURITIES
(tightly)   (openly)

Red: "You can't go around just trusting everyone you see. It doesn't matter how I feel anyway. What really matters is the issue at hand. Why do we always end up talking about feelings and garbage no one can do anything about anyway?!"

Blue: "I just want to feel close to you. I need you to know how special and important you are to me. Can't we ever forget business and talk about us. We used to dream about our future together and feel close. I'm so scared we won't make it in our marriage. I don't feel like a good parent anymore. And I know I haven't been a good spouse to you either."

Red: "You are making mountains out of molehills. Of course, I love you. Now let's stop talking about things we can't resolve. You knew who I was when you married me so what's the big deal?"

Blue: "I just want to spend more time with you and get to know you better. I want you to know me and understand my feelings."

Blue husband concerning Red wife:

I have come to the conclusion that she either is totally void of feelings or totally insecure and afraid that whoever gets inside her head won't like her when they really find out who she is in there.

Red wife's inward thoughts:

Showing my feelings is a sign of weakness. I am not weak and, therefore, I will never show any feelings. Besides, people might use them against me later on.

or

What is the big deal with feelings. You should know how I feel. I must love you. I married you didn't I?!

HIGH PRODUCTIVITY   versus   STRONG PERFECTIONISM

Red: "If a job's worth doing, let's stop talking and get it done."

Blue: "If a job's worth doing at all, it's worth doing right."

Reds want to complete the task while Blues want the task to be perfect before completion. This is most frustrating in a Red-Blue relationship, because both people are highly committed to productivity, but they rarely agree on the quality of the finished product or the necessary timelines. Particularly noticeable times of conflict are experienced when packing for vacations, having friends over for dinner, or completing a project at work.

Red: (driven by productivity) "I feel like my reputation is at stake for every deadline I miss."

Blue: (driven by perfectionism) "I feel like my name is on every article of clothing I sew."

LOGICAL (unemotional)   versus   EMOTIONAL (irrational)

Dialogue between Red employer and Blue employee:

Red: "Why you do what you do is totally insignificant to me. Just perform."

Blue: "Why would I perform for someone who doesn't care about why I do what I do?"

Red: "How I feel about you has nothing to do with how well you should perform."

Blue: "How you feel about me has everything to do with how well I perform."

Red: "Look, just do your job well and everything will be fine."

Blue: "Look, just appreciate me and tell me how well I'm doing my job and everything will be just fine."

One couple was distressed when the Red wife wouldn't intercede in arguments between the Blue father and Blue daughter. "If you loved me," he would say, "you would stand up for me. For no other reason than the fact that I'm the parent, you should defend me." The Red wife was furious that he would try and force her to referee between her two emotional "children." Reds quickly tire of other's emotional baggage and the need to be loved and told so all the time.

Blues usually feel betrayed by Reds emotionally. One Blue wife tearfully said, after twenty-five years of marriage to a Red husband, "Last night I had the best evening of our entire marriage... My eight year old daughter and I went out shopping and to the movies."

Reds typically feel traumatized by Blues taking everything personally. Reds appear insensitive (and often are), but they speak their mind directly and mean no malicious harm with their directness.

"Just remember that if I fire you, your work is unacceptable. Otherwise, carry on and know I am pleased," says the Red employer. The Blue appreciates hearing daily about the quality of the work and the reassuring sense of security on the job. Reds tire quickly of all the emotional needs of Blues. The less the

Blues get reassurance, the greater their need becomes to receive it.

INSENSITIVE   versus   TOO SENSITIVE

An evening out:

Blue: "Do you think what I'm wearing will be appropriate for the party tonight?"

Red: "Don't ask me again whether I like the dress you're wearing. It's fine. If I didn't like it, I'd ask you to wear something else."

Philosophical differences:

Blue: "Life's a bitch and then you die."

Red: "If you continue to bitch, you're going to die."

Twenty years later:

Blue: "I was three months pregnant with our third child. I felt fat and ugly and you still forced me to have sex with you."

Red: "This is ridiculous. That was twenty years ago. Are you still whining about that?"

Blue: "I've never forgiven you for forcing yourself on me when I felt so ugly and fat."

Red: "Just because you were three months pregnant, and felt ugly and fat, didn't necessarily mean my sex drive ceased to exist too."

IMPATIENT   versus   IMPATIENT, BUT LONG
                                                         SUFFERING

Blue parent to child:

"I want you to clean your room right now. We are not going to live like pigs. I clean the house every day so we can have a nice environment and you need to help too. It seems like nobody works around here but me and I'm sick and tired of doing it all. If you can't get your room cleaned, then don't ask me to do anything for you."

Note: Other personalities call this the "Blue Lecture." It usually lasts anywhere from five minutes to an hour depending on the degree of the Blue's need to be understood.

Red parent to child:

"If you expect to be breathing in five minutes, your room had better be clean."

INTENSE

Everything is a big deal in Red-Blue relationships. They care deeply and commit strongly to life. Neither takes a back seat to the other. Both have terrific concentration. Reds exude a more powerful verbal intensity, while Blues create a gritty non-verbal intensity. It's much like watching a Martina Navratilova versus Chris Evert-Lloyd tennis match. Both players are verbally and non-verbally dynamic. Both players are intense and focused.

UNFORGIVING, BUT MOVES ON	versus	UNFORGIVING AND RESENTS

Blues remember *everything* that ever happened in a relationship. They feel the same joy or anger that they felt twenty years before. They scar deeply and do not forgive easily. They withhold affection and genuine intimacy because of their resentment. In their hearts, Reds don't forgive any more than Blues. Intellectually, their head simply helps them move on and more efficiently cope with life. Speaking of her thirty year anniversary cruise to Alaska with her Red husband, one Blue wife resentfully remarked, "We never had a real honeymoon. So it's about time he showed me a good time. We'll have a great second honeymoon whether he likes it or not!"

POSSESSIVE

Both are prone to jealously and control. Both love with strings attached. "What's in it for me?" is a common concern they share. Both need to know they are number one in the relationship. Reds are more possessive of things, while Blues are more possessive of people.

REBELLIOUS	versus	BEHAVED

Driving in a car to work:

Blue: "The speed limit is 55 miles per hour and that is precisely what I intend to go."

Red: "Rules were made for people. People weren't made for rules!"

Blue: "People made the rules and people should follow the rules the people they elect make. Besides, it saves lives."

Red: *"Your* driving will never save lives. I have an important meeting to get to on time."

Blue: "If no one obeyed the law, think of the chaos we would have."

Red: "If people would just use their brain and think a little when they drive we wouldn't need these ridiculous laws. I don't need them because I'm a thinking driver."

In a work setting:

I remember a working relationship I once shared with two men (one Red and one Blue). The Blue would constantly question whether our supervisor would approve the decision we were making and the Red would constantly promote the idea of doing first and asking questions later. The Blue personality saw the Red as too rebellious and the Red personality saw the Blue as too behaved. Both offered a terrific balance to the team. Blues tend to see the barbed wire on the top of the fence. Reds see the holes underneath.

RESPONSIBLE

Both personalities are highly dependable. They take commitment seriously and act accordingly. Neither tolerates irresponsibility well. Both are highly principled. Reds are fiercely loyal to causes, while Blues are fiercely loyal to people.

ACHIEVER

Both are regarded as tremendous task-masters. They work hard throughout their lives to succeed. Both give work a high priority. (Play is always secondary to Reds and Blues.) Reds often achieve best through others and Blues achieve best through themselves. Blues are perfectionistic and detail conscious, while Reds are more leadership prone with strong skills in motivation and production. Both do best when allowed to operate within the limits they set for themselves. They are always stretching themselves professionally, but often for different reasons.

INTIMIDATING

Reds and Blues share the dubious honor of being perceived as intimidating. Both intimidate each other. Blues are so good at what they do, that they intimidate Reds. Reds are so logical and verbal that they intimidate Blues. Both recognize their unique skill level and can be highly cooperative or terribly destructive. Choosing to win by intimidation is hardly a recommended style for successful relationships. Reds and Blues are often unaware of how they intimidate each other. Consequently, each blames the other for poor communication. Neither is particularly sympathetic to the other's personality. Both remain somewhat aloof and justified in their intimidating style.

CRITICAL OF OTHERS   versus   CRITICAL OF SELF
                                                    AND OTHERS

When an issue arises, the general consensus is that Reds will find the fault to lie with others while Blues tend to look for the fault within themselves. Reds do a lot of introspection but rarely in the public's eye. Blues are more willing to comment on their own inadequacies as well as others. Both personalities are highly critical and blame oriented. Neither is comfortable with unresolved mistakes.

ARROGANT   versus   SELF-RIGHTEOUS

Both feel they are right. Both critically judge each other without a moment's notice. Neither is quick to see their own shortcomings despite repeated remarks from others. Reds exude an arrogance which suggests that they know everything and are always right. Blues maintain a daily vigil of moral self-righteousness and piety, which tends to alienate Reds from comfortably connecting with them on any intimate level.

PROACTIVE   versus   NEGATIVE

Deadlocked in disagreement for exasperating periods of time, Reds and Blues tend to see problems with a critical eye as opposed to anticipating the possibilities. Reds move easier through the negative than Blues. However, in their movement, they often dump unnecessary negativity on those around them. Gloomy clouds can be noticed more often in the Red-Blue companionship. Neither knows how to play well. They usually depend on others to bring out whatever sunshine life has to offer. However, they are also capable of strong productivity and action which often pushes them through difficult impasses in the relationship.

DOESN'T LOVE EASILY, BUT STRONG COMMITMENT	versus	LOVES DEEPLY AND DISAP-POINTED BY THOSE WHO CAN'T LOVE. (maintains strong commitment)

Reds are amazingly loyal to relationships (personal and professional). They appear to be so distant and yet they are actually very committed to those they accept into their lives. Reds are not terribly personable with others and often seem quite detached from the world in general. Actually, they can be the finest friends. They can be deeply devoted to their families, as well.

Blues share the strong commitment the Reds feel for relationships. Blues love deeply and commit completely to their families, careers or whatever they deem valuable. Blues are generally devoted to relationships, despite the pain or disappointments the relationships may bring. Reds and Blues value responsible and committed relationships. Regardless of the quality, Blues find terminating relationships very difficult to do.

MAKING THE MOST OF UNCOMPLEMENTARY OPPOSITES

REDS NEED BLUES:	BLUES NEED REDS:
To teach them compassion	To teach them honest feedback
To soften their communication	To teach them assertiveness
To point out details	To get the job done
To promote them	To give them specific direction
To encourage their risk taking	To foster a sense of security
To plan the action	To execute the plan
To confront them directly	To understand them
To not take comments personally	To appreciate them
To approve of their style and direction	To include them in plans
To trust them	To be trustworthy

POTENTIAL CONFLICTS OF UNCOMPLEMENTARY OPPOSITES

REDS	BLUES
Power-oriented	Intimacy-oriented
Selfish	Selfless
Wants to look good	Wants to be good
Logical	Emotional
Insensitive	Compassionate
Productive	Creative
Tactless	Beats around the bush
Stubborn	Stubborn
Arrogant	Self-righteous
Direct and self-assured	Indirect and self-conscious

Fire and Ice

RED-WHITE RELATIONSHIPS

Red-White relationships are one of the most common combinations found among the personalities. They share many commonalities (i.e., power-orientation, self-serving, and need for respect). Interestingly, even their differences are often more supportive rather than distracting. For example, Reds like to lead and Whites enjoy following. The Red says "Me, Tarzan." The White replies, "Terrific, Jane sounds good to me!" The Red is impatient, and the White quite patient, which further complements the relationship. They accomodate each other's innate limitations and promote each other's natural strengths.

OVERVIEW

Red Personality	White Personality
MOTIVE	
Power	Peace
NEEDS	
to be right	power and control of self
to be respected	to be respected
to look good to others (academically)	to feel good within self
approval	acceptance
WANTS	
challenging adventure	secure excitement
leadership	protection
to please self	to please self and others
to hide insecurities (tightly)	to reveal insecurities
BEHAVIOR STYLE	
change	stability
high profile	low profile
high complexity	low complexity
controlling	neither seeks control or to be controlled
unemotional	feels deeply, finds expression of feelings difficult

Red Personality	White Personality
logical	logical
direct communication (with facts)	direct communication (with facts)
delegator	doer
impatient	patient
demanding	non-demanding
tense	relaxed
possessive	non-possessive (unless threatened)
confrontive	non-confrontive
strong verbal	strong non-verbal
manipulative	subtly manipulative
can't love easily, but strong commitment	loves easily and strong commitment
high productivity	consistent producer
defiant of rules	compliant with rules
tactless	tactful
gives advice and expects compliance	gives advice only when asked
does not seek advice	accepts advice freely
intimidating	intimidating
critical of others	tolerant of others
arrogant	feels inadequate
gives others guilt	feels a lot of guilt
unforgiving but moves on	forgiving, but remembers
innovative	creative
negative	overwhelmed
obsessive-compulsive	dedicated only when interested
difficult to share feelings with	easy to talk to, hard to get feelings from
poor listener	excellent listener
blames others	blames self
insensitive	too sensitive
achiever	lazy
lies to save face	lies to avoid repercussion
rebellious	subversive

INTERPERSONAL RELATIONSHIPS

(In-depth Presentation)

POWER   versus   PEACE

The different motives of these personalities are effectively illustrated in a married relationship between a Red wife and a White husband. She was furious with him one morning due to a conversation they were having. She wanted to be right in the worst way and he wouldn't accomodate her. She suddenly jumped up from her chair at the kitchen table where they were having cereal, picked up her bowl of Wheaties and smashed it against the floor. In order to preserve whatever peace he could muster into the relationship at this point, the husband began picking up the broken pieces and emptying them into the trash can. Noticing that he was more interested in keeping peace than acquiescing to her superior intellect, she stormed back into the kitchen and poured milk all over the Wheaties. Then she ordered him to leave the kitchen until the milk and Wheaties had dried on the floor, making it far more difficult to clean up.

She laughed hysterically as she told the story. "Who eventually did clean up the mess?" I asked. "Well, he did, of course," she mocked. I still have visions of this fifty-five year old man stooping over a dried mess of cereal and milk, and cleaning it up in order to facilitate peace. They both got what they wanted. She felt powerful and he was at peace.

TO BE RESPECTED

Both seek respect in different ways. The Reds expect to be accomodated. The Whites expect to be left alone. Both enjoy distinct time frames and work styles, and continually seek methods for protecting their preferences. Whites are more vulnerable to feeling a lack of respect due to their own diminished self-esteem than Reds. Whites handle how Reds show respect better than any other personalities do. They often take them with a little tongue in cheek. One White husband told me, "I'm the boss around the house. My wife gave me permission to say that."

CHALLENGING ADVENTURE   versus   SECURE EXCITEMENT

Reds thrive on adventure. They love the opportunity to risk physical danger. My Red daughter constantly tries to upgrade her ability to handle the fast and scary rides at amusement parks. From an early age she experienced thrills from unique adventures. Whites also enjoy excitement, but prefer the assurance of support systems and/or guidelines. Police officers tend to be primarily Red and White personalities. They thrive on the adventure and excitement offered by this occupation.

LEADERSHIP	versus	PROTECTION

Remember, "Me, Tarzan;" "Okay by me, I'll be Jane"? Both are quite comfortable with the roles of leader and follower in a Red-White relationship. The only problem comes if one or the other chooses to switch roles. It typically comes later in life, if at all. A committed couple or parent-child relationship could potentially experience great difficulty with the change.

One White woman let her Red husband give her a list to do every day for fifteen years, until she decided enough was enough and started ripping up his lists. Despite her change, he couldn't break the habit of list-making for six months.

Another individual let her Red husband make all the decisions. She would then quietly determine whether she liked the decisions he made or not. If he hadn't measured up to her standards (i.e. big enough house, enough money, successful friends) she became disappointed in him. She eventually was able to see how unfair it was to seek his financial protection and social leadership while casting all blame his direction when he performed beneath her standards.

CHANGE	versus	STABILITY

Red adolescents are constantly telling me they would rather be dead than live the boring lifestyle their parents live. "Can you imagine popping popcorn every night and just sitting around to talk?"

Reds are more willing to risk without a secured position in life than Whites are. Whites will risk but must first have both feet firmly on the ground. They are less certain of themselves and typically prefer the comforts of safe, familiar surroundings. Whites don't require the constant action Reds do. Both offer a comfortable blend for each other.

HIGH PROFILE	versus	LOW PROFILE

Red: "I've got things to do, places to go, and people to see."

White: "What things, why so many places, and must we see all the people?"

Whites make excellent traveling companions because they are perfectly contented to "go along for the ride." They are easily entertained. They don't like to be on stage like their Red friends. Reds are more driven to see it all and experience everything before they're too old to move.

CONTROLLING	versus	NEITHER SEEKS CONTROL OR TO BE CONTROLLED

The best example of this difference can be found in the world political scene. We have the U.S.S.R. representing the Red. They are a forceful nation with a history of invading other countries and controlling governmental policies throughout the world. Right next door to this powerful Red nation lies an equally powerful, yet totally different nation which represents the Whites. It is Finland. Finland seeks neither to control other nations nor to be controlled by them. They make life very difficult for any nation that tries to control them. They are a peace-loving land with a strong sense of pride. The U.S.S.R. is reflective of the Red personality, promoting its philosophies throughout the world with the obvious belief that they are right and what they believe should be espoused by all. So it goes with individual relationships as well.

LOGICAL

Both Reds and Whites have the capacity to be very logical. Both can be very shrewd. Reds are often locked predominantly in this mode of thinking, while Whites are capable of operating quite successfully on either an emotional or logical level. Due to their natural capacity to deal well with logic, Red-White relationships can enjoy hearty discussions on a broad base of topics. Strongly related to this is the Red's ability to communicate directly with facts while Whites can do it with facts and feelings. Subsequently, they make a good pair because the Reds stimulate the conversations and the Whites clarify and encourage a feeling tone in the conversations.

DELEGATOR	versus	DOER

Reds are most comfortable in a delegating role. They give orders well. They allow others to do the job once it is delegated. They promote individuality. Whites appreciate this freedom. Whites accomplish numerous things that others will never know about. They do not broadcast their activities like Reds often do. They simply carry out assignments and personal interests in a comfortable, casual style. Neither seems to mind the other's style. They respect their differences and appreciate that neither is receptive to changing for others so why waste the time or energy trying?!!!

IMPATIENT   versus   PATIENT

Whites quietly explain away a Red's temper. It is as if it isn't a real big issue to them. They seem to take it in the stride of a tourist at Yellowstone expecting to see "Old Faithful" errupting on schedule. They aren't particularly shaken by it. While they are not pleased with it, Whites appear to be less concerned with the Red's impatience than other personalities. Whites believe that everything comes to he who waits.

Reds get the job done. Whites quietly assume the role of friend and supporter. Sometimes Reds are unfairly criticized because of their impatient natures. One woman told me how unfair she had been in judging her parents, but couldn't resolve her feelings of favoritism for her (White) father over her (Red) mother. "Dad was so poorly equipped for life," she said. "He couldn't hold down a job and when he finally landed one, he wouldn't leave on vacation for fear it would be gone when he returned. One summer, my (Red) mother simply packed us all in the car and took us to Yosemite for a two week vacation. Despite her obvious concern for our well-being, I hated her then and I still don't enjoy her company today. It seems that she had no spirit or soul to her. It was all performance and obligation—tense performance at that. Somehow, my father taught me to dream and love and feel. When he died, I lost a very patient, understanding friend. I felt abandoned even though I was left in the very capable care of my mother."

DEMANDING   versus   NON-DEMANDING

My favorite quote on Red's perception of White's ability to assert themselves came from a powerful Red lawyer who was frustrated with his passive White wife who was trying to assert herself in their marriage. He was particularly upset one day and commented, "Living with her is like living with a person who has read a book on self-assertion with half the pages already ripped out." Reds find it difficult to contend with Whites when they initially become more demanding in the relationship. However, they quickly learn to appreciate the heightened interaction and the relationship often improves with this change.

Reds are the most verbally demanding of the personalities. Whites are the least verbally demanding. Red parents have strong expectations of their children. Red employers have strong expectations of their employees. White children and employees are often the best equipped to deal wih the strong demands of the Reds. Whites simply tend to accept the relationship as it is and don't demand much of the other person.

Particularly frustrating for Reds is the lack of goal setting done by Whites in the relationship. Reds are so goal-oriented that they expect everyone else to be also. Whites are often comfortable floating through life, while Reds want predetermined action plans. Whites do not see the need to set goals and rarely follow through as tenaciously as the Reds. This can be annoying to both personalities who seem to be most comfortable on the opposite ends of this spectrum.

STRONG VERBAL   versus   STRONG NON-VERBAL

It is great fun to watch the Red and White personalities in a power duel. It is often difficult to determine the "winner." Reds verbalize their position, while Whites express themselves non-verbally. In the long run, it is a toss up as to who is actually stronger. Most intriguing, however, is their *style* of presentation. It reminds me most of animals in nature. Remember the hunter and the hunted. Who really gets the best of the other? It's hard to tell.

One loving White mother quietly held her vigilance with an arrogant Red son who ditched school, experimented with the drug scene, and ran away from home. She quietly asserted her position regarding his choices. He continued to verbally lash out at life and all those intimately connected with him. Eventually, he chose to turn away from the drug scene and re-establish himself in school and home. I asked him what changed his mind. He said, "Have you ever felt like you were running in a marathon and there was a guy right next to you, competing with you, but giving you constant moral support and always stopping to get you water from the sidelines? No matter what I did, I couldn't shake her. She wore me out until I finally decided she knew a better way to run the race of life than I did."

DOES NOT   versus   ACCEPTS ADVICE
SEEK ADVICE   FREELY

Reds and Whites differ in their approach to advice. Reds simply do not often seek advice. Whites don't seek advice as much as they simply accept advice. Due to their quiet ways, Whites appear to be needing advice and protection. Generally speaking, Whites are far more inclined to be receptive to advice than Reds, especially when it is offered in kindness.

CRITICAL OF OTHERS   versus   TOLERANT OF OTHERS

Most Reds are judgmental, while their White companions innately find themselves highly tolerant. Very few things bring Whites to criticism, while Reds find numerous behaviors of others to be unacceptable. Reds often voice their disapproval which drives others away from developing an intimate relationship while Whites invite others to share and willingly support differences of opinion.

One White patient was mortified when her Red boyfriend almost started a fist fight with a man who parked too close to his car. She was embarrassed by his public display of anger and felt his criticism was totally inappropriate. She even threatened to leave the car and walk home if he didn't just get in the car and drive away. He felt justified because the other guy had no business parking so close and someone had to tell him. (Who better than a Red, right?!) She felt it was just one more unnecessary confrontation that was undeserving of his constantly critical eye.

ARROGANT   versus   FEELS INADEQUATE

One White woman felt so inadequate and immoral (she had a child out of wedlock) that she married the first guy she met who loved her and role modeled strong character. (She was looking for his noble character to make up for her lacking morality. She was hoping his love for her would increase her love for herself.) She selfishly married this man and dutifully gave him eighteen years of wedded bliss, masking all her true feelings and never looking within herself to uncover the real hatred she felt for her "spineless, immoral self." We met in therapy after she had fallen in love with another man and had an affair only to discover that she no longer could live with her husband because she didn't love him. (Naturally, she had *never* loved him. She had used him to make her feel better about herself.) She wasn't a "spineless, immoral person" at all. She was a wonderful, capable human being who had made some poor choices. Rather than see herself accurately, she found an easier way. She found a husband who loved himself and her and would willingly cover all her "inadequacies." Three children later, she woke up and saw herself for the wonderful person she truly was and now the price for originally taking this "easier route" is a devastated husband, three frustrated children, betrayed extended family and friends. The price is much higher than it would have been had she been able to raise her self-image and accept herself (and her poor choices) earlier in life.

Reds often distance themselves in this wonderful world of emotions with their arrogance. They often miss true friendship because one cannot be intimate with someone who is better or less than them. (Intimacy requires equality.) Arrogance is a shallow defense of a rich treasure which lies hidden in the heart of Reds. Either they discard this shallow, pitiful defense and let themselves know intimacy and vulnerability or they remain a prisoner for life in their own self-constructed cells. At times, I wonder if the passivity of Whites enables Reds to continue their denial. Yet, a White's patience and acceptance may be the most effective method for eventually enticing the Red's emotions to the surface.

GIVES OTHER GUILT   versus   FEELS A LOT OF GUILT

He was one of the kindest men I have ever met in a therapeutic session. He looked so lost and forelorn. He began our session telling about his precious daughter, Linda, who had repeatedly rattled her crib as early as one year old to get her way. She was Red—demanding all the time. Over the years, she rebelled against their standards, got into drugs, ditched school, slept around and eventually ran away from home.

On one occasion, he and his (Red) teenaged son were called from the therapists office and told to forcibly take her from his office to a treatment center down the coast. They complied. She was furious and in her rage spit in her (White) father's face as he restrained her in the back seat. He did nothing to retaliate. She turned to her (Red) brother on the other side and began to do the same to him. He calmly, and almost hoping to be defied, said, "Just try it, sweetheart, and you'll never be able to spit again." She was furious, so she turned back at her father and spit at him.

I asked him why he allowed her to behave as she did. He told me he felt so guilty that he couldn't blame her for spitting. I asked him what he had done that made him feel so guilty and he couldn't come up with anything. Still he felt guilty. She used this on him her whole life. She knew her (Red) brother wouldn't take it so she gave it to her guilt-ridden (White) dad.

At one point she shared a bathroom with her brother. She smoked and he told her never to do so in the bathroom. She ignored him and did so anyway. One day he simply took her ashtray from the bathroom and spread all the ashes out on her sheets and remade the bed. She never smoked in their bathroom again. The father seemed pleased that his son could counter the daughter so effectively but was unable or unwilling to challenge her in the same way. Given the green light by her father, a most immature Linda continued to give her father the blame for her messed-up life.

OBSESSIVE-COMPULSIVE   versus   DEDICATED ONLY WHEN INTERESTED

Reds usually become obsessed about everything with which they connect. They resemble a young teenager who hooks up with every new fad that comes along. Whether it's food, sports, religion, or whatever, Reds are known to take extreme stands. It is hard to deter them. They can overeat with the same vigor that they arise at 6:00 a.m. to hit a little white ball into holes on green grass. Whatever the obsession, they are compulsive about it. Whites are able to commit just as deeply, but feel very little compulsion to tenaciously follow through. They are, however, equally tenacious when they feel the dedication. Bjorn Borg, who appears to be a White personality, reigned as the king of tennis until he lost interest. He didn't even try to regain the desire. He simply quit. Reds are more inclined to reassert themselves and force the desire to be there in order to accomodate the obsession.

POOR LISTENER   versus   EXCELLENT LISTENER

Reds generally prefer debates rather than casual conversation. Whites are most comfortable simply hearing what others have to say. Reds are so certain that they know everything that they don't often deem it necessary to pay full attention to details in conversations. They are more concerned with giving advice and getting results. Feelings are less important than facts. One (Red) father was more interested in the future problems his overweight, (White) daughter would have "landing a husband' than her feelings of low self-esteem from her current weight condition.

People often seek out Whites for their patience and gentle manner in discussing differences. They are willing to give the time that is necessary to fully understand another individual. Whites are truly interested in other's feelings and life situations. They like being included in other's lives and freely give the time necessary in promoting warm, communicative relationships.

MAKING THE MOST OF COMPLEMENTARY OPPOSITES

REDS NEED WHITES:	WHITES NEED REDS:
To calm them in crisis	To motivate them
To listen to them	To inspire and encourage them
To bounce ideas off	To lead them
To feel safe with	To share risks with
To promote compromise	To organize them
To delegate responsibility	To promote them
To support them	To establish healthy boundaries
To balance them with perspective	To provide vision
To remind about quality versus quantity	To stay task-oriented
To communicate logically with	To set goals and objectives

POTENTIAL CONFLICTS OF COMPLEMENTARY OPPOSITIES

REDS	WHITES
Too demanding	Too accepting
Arrogant	Self-doubting
Bossy	Passive
Too opinionated	Uncommited
Always right	Easily walked on
Verbally stubborn	Silently stubborn
Often promotes conflict	Promotes peace at all costs
Always telling	Always asking
Tactless and rude	Craves kindness
Workaholic	Lazy

Friendly Fire

RED-YELLOW RELATIONSHIPS

This combination of personalities is a vibrant one. Reds and Yellows enjoy verbal banterings and enjoy the freedom from most emotional garbage and heavy sentiments experienced by other personalities. They are adventurous and dynamic, often amazing and amusing friends with their zest for living and many accomplishments. They are unique in the playfulness of the Yellow and the productivity of the Red. They differ slightly with the self-centeredness of the Yellow and the selfishness of the Red. However, the obvious commonality is their preference of first looking out for number one—themselves.

They are both highly motivated in life. I would guess that suicide ranks lower with this combination than any other. They seem to value themselves and feel a commitment to new experiences and challenges in life. They are both excited about change and find little need to be concerned with stability.

Interestingly, this combination is rare among committed, married couples. It is, however, rather common among friends. Both maintain a healthy perspective of each other. This personality combination reminds me of a white-water river rafting trip—carefree, yet productive, filled with adventure, excitement, and occasional moments of passion.

OVERVIEW

Red Personality	Yellow Personality
MOTIVE	
Power	Fun
NEEDS	
to be right	intimacy
to be respected	to be praised
to look good to others (academically)	to look good to others (socially)
approval	approval
WANTS	
challenging adventure	playful adventure
leadership	freedom
to please self	to be noticed
to hide insecurities (tightly)	to hide insecurities (loosely)
BEHAVIOR STYLE	
likes change	likes change

high profile	high profile
high complexity	low complexity
controlling	craves freedom
unemotional	emotional
logical	logical
direct communication (with facts)	direct communication (with facts and feelings)
delegator	delegator/performer
impatient	good natured
demanding	obnoxious
intense	carefree
possessive	non-possessive
confrontive	avoids confrontation
strong verbal	strong verbal
manipulative	seeks escape
can't love easily, but strong commitment	loves easily, but poor commitment
high productivity	scattered productivity and playfulness
defiant of rules	defiant of rules
tactless	tactless (with humor)
gives advice and expects compliance	gives advice, but unconcerned with compliance
does not seek advice	welcomes positive advice from others
intimidating	inviting
critical of others	accepting of others
arrogant	vain
gives others guilt	rarely gives or takes guilt
unforgiving but moves on	forgiving
innovative	innovative
negative	positive
obsessive-compulsive	lacks discipline

difficult to share feelings with	easy to share feelings with
poor listener	poor listener
blames others	blames others
conflict oriented	avoids conflict
lies to save face	lies to save face and not disappoint
expects a lot, unappreciative	appreciative
consistent	inconsistent
determined	unthinking/naive

INTERPERSONAL RELATIONSHIPS

(In-depth Presentation)

Red Personality   **Yellow Personality**

POWER   versus   FUN

She knew he was powerful when she married him. He had enjoyed a most successful career in the oil business. He showered her with gifts and kept her heart spinning with numerous romantic intimacies. She was like sunshine in his life. Full of warmth, she radiated happiness and excitement. She represented everything he had bypassed in order to be successful in his hard-driving career. She felt he was more committed to her than he had ever been to his career. She was right about being more committed to her than his career. However, she forgot just how committed he had always been, and still was, to himself. One day he invited her to take a leisurely drive in their convertible Rolls Royce and enjoy a picnic on the beach. She was thrilled with this playful gesture. When he began driving in a different direction, she became somewhat suspicious. Before long, his selfish plan became more evident. They were headed for his mother's. This Red man despised his mother but felt obligated to periodically visit her and did so only with his colorful Yellow wife, who could carry the conversation. He was still looking out for himself. The fun possibilities of the picnic were quickly discarded for the more selfish motive of meeting his personal obligations of visiting his mother.

Yellows often frustrate the Reds with their disorganization as much as Reds frustrate Yellows with their obsession with power. Taking charge of one's life is a cornerstone of personal power. Yellows usually fail to understand the importance of personal power and being responsible. Reds have no problem dissecting problems and making sense out of their lives. They are direct and enjoy having control over everything they do. Yellows infuriate Reds with their casual concern with financial matters, social obligations and protocol. They are more interested in sharing time with fascinating people who laugh than people who are in control of their lives. Reds enjoy control and find no personality more impossible to control than Yellows. Like a winged bird in flight, they simply take off and land when they feel like it. Reds often resent this frivolity and feel their all-important power threatened by the casual mockery Yellows often display for them.

TO BE RESPECTED   versus   TO BE PRAISED

Reds are far more concerned with being respected, while Yellows are typically willing to abdicate respect or power in search of attention. Reds are always looking out for themselves while Yellows are hoping *others* are looking out for them. The Reds want to produce the movie and earn the money while the Yellows want to be on stage and earn the audience's praise.

Reds don't often compliment others well. In fact, they are generally quite uncomfortable with giving and/or receiving compliments. Jobs needing to be done should be done with little fanfare in a Red's estimation. Yellows couldn't disagree more. They compliment easily and sincerely. The love to be acknowledged. Perhaps the greatest driving need in Yellows with regard to interpersonal relationships is that of being praised. They rarely receive it from their Red companions. Numerous unnecessary family arguments actually stem from Red parents neglecting to praise Yellow children. Red employers miss an easy incentive when they neglect to compliment Yellow employees.

Reds only demand respect. For them, respect is more tangible than praise. Reds ask to be seen as the experts, the leaders, the knowledgeable ones. They will return the favor tenfold. Reds and Yellows have very different needs. Both must learn much from each other in order to effectively appreciate their different styles.

TO LOOK GOOD TO   versus   TO LOOK GOOD TO
OTHERS (academically)   OTHERS (socially)

Looking good is desired by both Reds and Yellows. Perhaps nothing allies them more than this motive of hiding their inadequacies in order to appear good on the surface. Reds and Yellows struggle with intimacy because they prefer not to risk themselves emotionally in relationships. Reds are more direct in their defensive posture of guarding their feelings. They are not coy or innocent in their rejection of sharing themselves. Yellows appear innocent and often invite others in with brash openness. However, they also resist true intimacy. Yellows remind me of deer in the forest. They are beautiful to see, but if you come too close they quickly disappear in the foliage which covers and protects them. Yellows instinctively focus the conversation on others. They often find it very difficult to talk about their true feelings because they fear other's judgement. Without a trained eye, people often fall right into the trap and spend an evening or even a lifetime with Yellows discussing intimacies but never actually being intimate at all.

Perhaps the element most lacking in this combination is emotional depth. Neither caters to the needs of others. Both struggle with intimacy. Together, Reds and Yellows have a most difficult time admitting their inadequacies. They must also work very diligently to overlook each other's inadequacies rather than remembering them for later debate and teasing. Yellows are more likely to expose themselves but neither risks freely at the truly intimate level. Both require patience and trust in order to free themselves of their most closely guarded treasures—their insecurities.

APPROVAL

It is interesting that both of the more verbal personalities seek approval while the more passive personalities seek acceptance. Yellows and Reds seek approval for completely different reasons. Yellows seek approval to know they are socially desirable. They do not appear to value their own opinion as much as they do the opinion of others. Reds are typically impressed with the social skills of Yellows. Reds want approval for their intellectual prowess. They need to know that others approve of them academically. Yellows find approval of Red's intellectual capacity easy to give. What they struggle with is the arrogant style Reds often use to present themselves.

CHALLENGING ADVENTURE   versus   PLAYFUL ADVENTURE

No other personality combination can begin to compete with the adventurous spirit of a healthy Red-Yellow team. They are willing to forego many of life's luxuries in order to travel the world, risk personal danger and experience new opportunities. They are known to be constantly remodeling, going back to school, traveling, attending plays, etc. They are terrifically spontaneous and proactive.

HIGH PROFILE

Red and Yellow personalities feel secure within themselves and open to new challenges and opportunities. They like visibility. They don't work behind the scenes of life but rather prefer to be "on stage." Both enjoy people and often find themselves challenging each other for the spotlight. Reds succeed in maintaining their high profile with knowledge, hard work, and leadership skills. Yellows succeed in maintaining their high profile with innate love for people, charismatic style, and positive energy.

CONTROLLING   versus   CRAVES FREEDOM

Picture in your mind a determined Red mother racing after a runaway Yellow toddler who has escaped through the open front door. Reds want to control most people's destiny. Yellows want the right to determine their own destiny. Whenever Yellows feel their freedom is being challenged, they resist. Reds often frustrate themselves trying to channel a Yellow's zest for life. Both are benefitted by each other's perceptions of how to live life. Reds offer responsibility. Yellows offer intrigue. Both see their roles in relationships very differently. Successful blending requires an acceptance of each other's perspective.

UNEMOTIONAL   versus   EMOTIONAL

Yellows can live without the depth of emotional connection Blues require but they are often stunned—unprepared for the limited expression Reds display. One Yellow husband shouted at his Red wife, "I would love to see you just once break down and show your real feelings. You are stoic. It's like getting water out of a stone. I give up! I really do! No human can be that *inhuman!!*"

Reds are quite accepting of a Yellow's emotionally charged displays. Reds appreciate their emotional excitement. Upon retirement, one Red employee shared with his Yellow colleague, "Well, I do have to say this about you. You are definitely 'one-of-a-kind.' I have never met anyone as vivacious and emotionally charged as you seem to be about life."

LOGICAL

Perhaps the saving grace in Red-Yellow relationships from a Red's perspective is the Yellow's ability to reason. Reds are so capable with their reasoning power that they rely heavily on the other person's ability to meet them on their turf. Yellows can do just that. Both personalities are skilled at debating issues without necessarily resorting to emotional drama. They share strong verbal skills. Reds and Yellows enjoy the pleasure of boldly debating opposite points of view and remaining personally unscathed. Both are rather direct with their communication. Their relationship is unique in that it relies on their mutual ability to reason.

DELEGATOR   versus   DELEGATOR/PERFORMER

No personality delegates across the board like the Reds. They are masterful in their ability to see the broad picture and select competent individuals to carry through on the details. Yellows share this ability to pass responsibilities on to others. They, too, are most comfortable with delegation and trusting that others will complete the job. Reds have the edge with regard to vision, while Yellows have the edge with regard to trust. Yellows do not struggle with control like Reds do. Like the pied piper, they charismatically entice others to follow their leadership.

In the long run, it is the Red that generally remains committed and successful in the position of leadership. They are decisive leaders who willingly focus themselves on task. Yellows typically prefer to perform somewhere in the organization or on their own. Managing others is often too demanding and unpleasant compared with hands-on performance. For example, a Yellow university professor who became a department chairman suddenly quit after only two years because he missed the opportunities of getting close to students and performing in the classroom. Preparing department agendas and fighting with university policy was more frustration than reward for him.

DEMANDING   versus   OBNOXIOUS

Yellows are often poor judges of character. They tend to be more concerned with having a good time than considering the possible negative consequences of running with unhealthy friends. One Yellow sixteen year old was acting up and frustrating his dominant Red father so much that the father ultimately demanded that his son change. "Why don't you give up this crazy attitude of yours, and tell your friends you are a businessman now and all you care to worry about is business transactions?!" he requested.

With all the diplomacy of a Yellow teenager, the son sarcastically replied, "Yeah, right dad! Now I'm a businessman. I only consider business transactions." Turning to me, as if I were one of his peers, he continued, "In the future it will be necessary for you to contact my social secretary to schedule any therapy sessions in order that we not conflict with business. This is necessary, in order to prevent any further disappointments for the chairman of the board, my father."

The next evening, he got drunk and fell asleep in his friend's car. The following morning he had to run three miles to get to work on time as a busboy at his father's restaurant. The more demanding the father became the more obnoxious the son grew. The more obnoxious the son grew the more demanding the father became.

There is a happy ending to this story. Reds and Yellows share the common need to look good to others. Father and son were able to come to a compromise that would enable them both to save face in the community and with the boy's friends.

INTENSE   versus   CAREFREE

Reds seem to care about everything while Yellows appear to care about nothing. Reds are very intense people (obsessive-compulsive), while Yellows are carefree and often undisciplined. Both represent opposing lifestyles. Reds tenaciously attack problems and hang on until they have a solution. Yellows freely release problems, convinced that most things are never truly resolved anyway so why get upset about something you can't control. Yellows often help others accept that Reds really are wonderful people who just get carried away with their convictions and forget the human element in life. Reds often move others (Yellows included) to action and create a sense of conviction.

Time and again we see the people skills of the Yellow and the task skills of the Red. Given mutual respect, they are highly complementary of each other.

POSSESSIVE   versus   NON-POSSESSIVE

Reds are typically very possessive of material goods and personal relationships. Yellows are the least possessive of the personalities. They love people and feel certain that they will be loved in return. Reds feel love is best displayed by responsible behavior and kept promises. They are typically unsure of other's love for them.

Sometimes the Yellow's lack of possessiveness is construed as not caring as much. This perception may hurt the feelings of those they encounter. Yellows tend to promote, "If you love someone, set them free; if they come back, they're yours; if not, they never were." Reds often read this passage differently. They are known to say, "If you love someone, set them free; if they don't come back, hunt them down and kill them."

MAKING THE MOST OF COMPLEMENTARY SIMILARITIES

REDS NEED YELLOWS:	YELLOWS NEED REDS:
To teach them charisma	To focus them
To converse logically	To praise them
To accept their leadership	To notice them
To cheerlead for them	To risk with them
To broaden their myopic vision	To give them freedom
To socialize them and idolize them	To allow for their spontaneity
To not take their criticism personally	To keep them on task
To be less scattered and inconsistent	To accept their boundless energy
To teach them spontaneity and laughter	To be positive and say "I'm sorry"

POTENTIAL CONFLICTS OF COMPLEMENTARY
SIMILARITIES

REDS	YELLOWS
Intense	Lighthearted
Workaholic	Playful orientation
Rude	Insensitive
Hide intimate feelings	Hide intimate feelings
Strong verbal argumentation skills	Strong verbal argumentation skills
Seek power	Seek intimacy
Factual and profound	Superficial chatterbox
Want to look good (intellectually)	Want to look good (socially)
Driven	Lack focused direction
Negative and critical	Positive and accepting

CHAPTER ELEVEN

The Blue Connections
Close and Comfortable
BLUE-BLUE RELATIONSHIP

Of all the colorful blends one finds in relationships, Blue-Blue combinations run the deepest emotionally and commit the longest. Blues are intimacy-based and with two Blues it is twice the commitment to sharing. Healthy Blues make the strongest commitment to their spouse in marriage. No other color marries itself with the success Blues do. Blue-Blue marriages are also the most common of same color marriages.

In the work force, Blues share perfectionistic tendencies and appreciate each other's dedication and commitment to quality work. Blues are loyal to people and respectful of authority. Blues trust Blues. They are reliable and conscientious. There is seldom any power struggle between Blues. The only exceptions to this come with unhealthy Blues who are fearful, hurt and angry from pervious encounters on the job. Bitter power plays and resentful comments often accompany these Blues. Typically, however, Blues focus on their own individual responsibilities and remain aloof from political havoc in the work setting.

This color combination usually enjoys warmth, sharing, sensitivity and quality relationships. They share many responsible traits important to successful relationships. They are often seen as role models for building meaningful connections with people. Blue-Blue interaction is sincere and committed. They share the unique values of integrity and intimacy.

SHARED INTIMACY

Blues value each other. No other color combination come by intimacy as naturally as Blue-Blue connections. When Blues are dating, or married, they do not take each other for granted after a while and start seeking personal hobbies to the exclusion of their companion. On the contrary, Blues are more interested in discovering activities they can enjoy together.

Blues understand that intimacy is not solely reflected by what goes on in the bedroom. They enjoy late dinner conversations about shared concerns. They appreciate physical touching and romantic glances with each other's eyes throughout the day. They sincerely care about each other's difficulties as well as happy celebrations. Blues understand the importance of remembering special occasions and mundane occasions as well. They innately think of each other and take time to demonstrate that they genuinely care.

Shared intimacy is their greatest strength. They feel the quality which comes from giving their relationship top priority. Blue-Blue combinations of all types (i.e., spouse, parent-child, siblings, colleagues, friends) value their relationship *most* and experience a natural depth other personality combinations must work hard to understand and achieve.

LOYALTY

Blues are loyal to each other. They are loyal to law and order. They are loyal to commitments. They are loyal to society's expectations. This shared loyalty makes their relationships very secure. Blue-Blue combinations are loyal to the person in the marriage, family, career or friendship—not merely loyal to the institution. For example, Blues commit to the happiness and personal development of their spouse rather than the religious or social obligation that comes with wedding vows and a marriage certificate. Blues care about the people in society. They don't just blindly accept and follow law and order or society's expectations. For example, Blues struggle with drunk drivers because Blues hurt for people whose lives are unjustly affected by people who drive under the influence of alcohol. Blue-Blue color combinations do remarkably well at keeping loyalty to each other in proper perspective and consciously committing to making it the significant priority in their life.

STRONG COMMITMENT

Whatever Blues commit to will succeed. They are a powerful team and willingly give time and effort to accomplishing everything they value. Blue-Blue parents are often seen as "too protective" because they appear to "overdo" everything from homework to curfew. By the time most kids become teenagers, they no longer suggest that their parents simply "overdo!" They now refer to their behavior as "overkill!"

Blues are focused and vulnerable to becoming myopic if they feed each other too much. One fourteen year old Yellow was exasperated with his Blue parents because they supported each other's perspective so readily that he felt unable to even present his case before they jointly overruled him. Piety and self-righteous attitudes can also out shine genuine commitment, if a moralistic approach is pursued. Blue-Blue combinations must be very careful not to feed each other's shared drive to the extent that other colors feel neglected, judged and/or abused.

On a positive note, Blue-Blue relationships experience a unique sense of commitment to each other. Patrick Henry was one of America's more successful founding fathers. His wife became mentally ill at the height of his career. Many believed he would have become the next President of the United States. He forsook it all to remain at home and offer his mentally ill wife the security of a loving and devoted husband until her death. Providing dignity for this woman, whom another might easily have abandoned in order to pursue their ambitions was so important to Patrick Henry. Discarding her in this final moment of life was unacceptable to such a sincerely committed Blue personality as evidenced by Patrick Henry.

APPRECIATION

Who appreciates a painting more than another painter? Blues give so much to everything they do, that they are most appreciated (which Blues crave) by other Blues. You know the phrase, "it takes one to know one." So it goes with Blues. They appreciate the quality in each other's work. They see the detail and recognize the time it takes to complete various work projects. They know the sacrifice Blues make to complete projects. They appreciate what few others even identify or understand.

PERFECTIONISM

Blue-Blue combinations do everything "above the call of duty." They believe "a job worth doing, is a job worth doing well." So how do colors respond to a unified Blue combination? They often mock them as "too perfectionistic" and "irritating" when working on a project. However, two Blues find each other's concern for detail very refreshing. They appreciate each other's commitment to quality. They usually value each other's opinion and expertise. Blue-Blue combinations can be found enjoying remodeling their house or taking classes together. They love to learn and improve themselves and their skills.

CARING COMMUNICATIONS

Blues turn off the television and talk. They enjoy meaningful conversations with each other. They often ask how each other's day went at work or home. They connect emotionally when they communicate. Blues take the time to really hear each other's feelings. They have tremendous empathy for each other and show concern for each other's tragedies as well as triumphs. They are sensitive to each other's moods and will talk into the early morning hours, if necessary, to understand each other's perspective.

PASSIONATE

Blues live for passion. They want to *feel* life rather than merely exist. Blues need to be involved in activities which count for something. They typically prioritize family and friends as most important. They are congruent with their priorities and subsequent behaviors. Unlike some personalities who claim to be very family-oriented and then spend their entire lives at the office or playing with friends, Blues typically spend their time and efforts in the same places they claim their priorities lie.

Obligation is significant but less vital to Blues than feelings. The letter of the law is less appealing than the spirit of the law. Blue-Blue combinations provide each other with a reason to be passionate. They care deeply and share intimately. They feel a personal sense of worth in simply being together. Their passion may come in the form of hobbies, career, family, friends or religion. Blue-Blue combinations promote passion within themselves by fostering a genuine concern for each other throughout their lives.

OBEDIENT

Blues are the most obedient of all personalities. Blue-Blue relationships do not struggle as most others do with defiance or resentment of authority. They generally accept law and order as important and follow rules without much difficulty. Both feel strongly about moral obligations and appreciate each other's commitment to high standards and rules.

TRUST

Blues are typically suspicious and lack trust in relationships. Not so with the

Blue-Blue color combination. Perhaps the reason they trust one another so easily is that neither person gives reason for the other to be suspicious. They usually share their feelings and communicate their goals, plans and daily activities. Subsequently, Blues trust each other and feel secure in the relationship.

DEPRESSION

Blues are not much help to each other when either is severely depressed. They don't have the necessary skills or attitude to demand change or cheer each other up. They typically "wait out" their companion's depression which is often counterproductive. One Red once said, "Blues are simply a waste of time." He was referring to their long suffering patience with each other, despite the negative implications of their depressive behavior.

PIOUS RIGIDITY

Blues can be very rigid in their self-righteousness. This deters their ability to be receptive to other people who see life differently or behave according to different standards. Blues can remain so aloof with their smugness in a relationship, that they get out of touch with others around them. This rigidity limits growth and intimacy with others outside the Blue-Blue connection.

INTENSITY

Blues are precise and determined in their lives. They approach every aspect of their lives with such intensity that both often experience burn-out and distress. Both feel so deeply for each other that they aren't much help in providing lighter moments of play or relaxation. Neither plays well or relaxes easily. It typically becomes necessary for them to turn outside of the relationship in order to find a more healthy and proper perspective.

QUALITY

Blues are typically very concerned about quality in their lives. They maintain high standards and expect the same from others. Blue-Blue relationships enjoy a level of quality few other combinations understand. Blues are generally willing to pay the price necessary for personal integrity. Blues often experience strong bonds of trust, sincerity and intimacy. They notice each other and see other's needs and concerns. I am reminded of my Blue daughter and her Blue Uncle Bill who spent a day at Disneyland together. We were celebrating Uncle Bill's birthday and after a full day at the amusement park, we sat down for pizza. On her own, my Blue daughter produced a special birthday card for her Uncle Bill, complete with stickers she secretly bought at Disneyland. She noticed his need and he appreciated her concern. They experienced a quality exchange. This awareness, combined with personal integrity, offer Blue-Blue color combinations the enviable prize of experiencing quality relationships.

Gentle Persuasion

BLUE-WHITE RELATIONSHIPS

Committed relationships come most frequently in "opposite packaging" (i.e., Reds with Whites and Blues with Yellows). The only exception to this rule of thumb lies in the common connection of Blue-White relationships. Perhaps the reason for this combination is the mutual sensitivity and compassion which both share.

Blues and Whites are both inclined to be concerned with feelings. Blues and Whites are low-key in their approach to each other. Interestingly, my experience indicates that Blue women are more inclined to become bored with White husbands, while Blue men are more appreciative of their White companion's accepting ways.

Major complaints Blues express of Whites are their non-committal ways, lack of initiative, and stubbornness. Whites are more likely to complain of Blues being controlling, too emotional, and unforgiving. Blues comment positively on the peaceful nature, kindness, willingness to listen, tolerance, and patience of Whites. Whites appreciate Blues for their sincerity, leadership and tactful assertion and loyalty.

The Blue-White relationship is an intriguing combination that willingly goes through life unnoticed. Healthy Blues are generally the spark plugs in these relationships, while *charactered* Whites offer a strong performance as supporting cast.

OVERVIEW

Blue Personality	White Personality
MOTIVE	
Intimacy	Peace
NEEDS	
to be understood	to be respected
to be appreciated	power and control of self
to be good for self (morally)	to feel good within self

acceptance   acceptance

WANTS

security   secure excitement
autonomy   protection
to please others   to please self and others
to reveal insecurities (openly)   to reveal insecurities

BEHAVIOR STYLE

high complexity   low complexity
doer (prefer autonomy)   doer (prefer direction)
controlling (power play)   neither seeks control
                                         or to be controlled
demanding   non-demanding
manipulative   subtle manipulation

stability   stability
emotional   emotional and logical
irrational (unrealistic expectations)   irrational (timid and fearful)
too sensitive (verbally)   too sensitive (non-verbally)
achiever   balanced

intense   relaxed
impatient   patient
critical of self and others   tolerant of others
blames self and others   blames self
unforgiving and resents   forgiving, but remembers

negative   overwhelmed
asserts self when necessary   non-assertive
confrontive   craves peace
willing to deal with conflict   avoids conflict
on principle
intimidating   intimidated

strong non-verbal   strong non-verbal
possessive   non-possessive (unless threatened)
compliant with rules   compliant with rules

tactful	tactful
behaved	behaved
obliging	obliging
emotionally responsible	emotionally irresponsible
gives advice and expects compliance	gives advice only when asked
seeks advice from experts	seeks advice freely
lies to avoid hurting others	lies to avoid conflicts and repercussion
self-righteous	feels inadequate
feels a lot of guilt	feels a lot of guilt
caring listener	excellent listener
direct communicator (with feelings)	indirect communicator (with feelings)
complex and deep when sharing feelings	easy to talk to; hard to get feelings from
loves deeply and has strong commitment	loves easily and has strong commitment

INTERPERSONAL RELATIONSHIPS

(In-depth Presentation)

Blue Personality   **White Personality**

INTIMACY   versus   PEACE

Blues generally prioritize initimacy as the most important component of every relationship. Whites place peace at the top of their list. Blues promote activities and opportunities which foster sharing. It is not uncommon for Blues to suggest taking a tennis lesson *together,* walks on the beach *together* or quiet conversation *together*. Whites appear receptive to accomodating the Blues' desires, if for no other reason than keeping the peace. Whites are very contented to pass the time alone or go places with others. Their need for togetherness is typically met long before Blue's needs are satisfied. Generally, their willingness to please others and "get along" is so important that Whites cooperate with their Blue companions.

Whites can quietly sabotage the intimacy needs of Blues, as well. One Blue woman was furious with her husband's unwillingness to get involved in much dialogue or shared decision-making. In desperation, she finally shouted, "I feel like I'm just talking to the wallpaper. Actually, he's not even strong enough to be considered wallpaper. He's more like the stuff inside the wall.".

Blues can nag and harass Whites until there is no peace. One White man who loved his fishing trips, had finally grown tired of his Blue wife's nagging about his annual fishing trip with the boys. "I don't know why she can't realize," he said, "that after all her shouting is over, I am going to do exactly what I planned to do in the first place. If she would just stop wasting our time by delaying my plans, we would both be better off."

What makes a Blue-White relationship work is the Blue's willingness to accept a White's peaceful style, and the White's willingness to share intimately with a Blue.

| TO BE GOOD FOR SELF (morally) | versus | TO FEEL GOOD WITHIN SELF |

Blues and Whites both need to feel good inside, but for very different reasons. Blues are driven by a moral conscience, while Whites are more concerned with distress. Blues willingly take on an issue of conflict if a principle is involved. Whites are more inclined to ignore a problem, regardless of the principle, if they perceive discomfort or distress resulting from the confrontation. Blues often resent the lack of involvement and moral commitment from White companions. Whites tend to resent persistent lecturing and moral demands of Blues.

| SECURITY | versus | SECURE EXCITEMENT |

"All I want is a solid million dollars in the bank and then I'll be more willing to risk another relationship with a woman," one Blue patient said. He represents the strong need Blues have for security, whether it be financial, emotional or physical. Whites are also inclined to seek security. However, they are more concerned with excitement than Blues. This additional twist entices them to pursue numerous risks that their Blue companions forego. Whites are often very quiet in expressing their need for excitement, but often seek situations which afford them opportunities for secure excitement. Blues are generally more comfortable in safer and similar surroundings, such as the security of known friends and family.

AUTONOMY	versus	PROTECTION

"Do Whites ever say anything without being asked?" a Blue father asked. "I can't believe how shallow our communication can be at times. I have to literally ask every possible question to get any answers. I would certainly appreciate a little cooperation, a little shared responsibility for the direction of our relationship.

Whites are basically followers. They go with the established direction of most conversations, peer situations and decisions. Basically, they are known to simply flow with life.

Whites generally accept being directed and protected by others. Their concern is simply *how* they are directed and protected. They are terribly resistant to demands or hostile control. Much like Afghanistan's resistance to Russia's brutal invasion, Whites resent the *style* of direction much more than the direction itself.

Blues, on the other hand, accept direction out of obligation and other appropriate expectations of relationships and societal pressures, but they prefer autonomy. Blues are typically not good team players. They will not accomodate others like Whites will. They do not want to lead anyone (including their White companions), which creates leadership problems for this personality combination. Blues are mostly committed to doing a job right, while Whites are more concerned with simply getting along. Neither personality prefers to lead, although Blues end up doing so in the majority of Blue-White relationships.

TO REVEAL INSECURI- TIES (openly)	versus	TO REVEAL INSECURI- TIES

One of this color combination's bonding of warmth is the vulnerability both Blues and Whites bring to the relationship. Throughout their lives, they share information and feelings which promote a closeness and trust few other combinations enjoy or understand. One man and woman were so successful in their ability to expose themselves to each other that eventually they fell in love because neither of them had ever achieved such openness with other relationships. Despite the fact that both tried dating others, the ability to trust was never the same. Eventually they married with the foundation of their relationship built on open communication and trust.

NOTE: Unhealthy Whites are known to appear vulnerable non-verbally, but they do not verbally share themselves. This presents a particularly frustrating dilemma for Blue companions who seek verbal sharing of intimacy (including insecurities).

HIGH COMPLEXITY   versus   LOW COMPLEXITY

Typically Blues are perceived to be more difficult to understand. Actually, both have clear needs. The Blues need to be understood and appreciated. The Whites need to feel in control of themselves and be respected. Whites operate on a power base, but seek peaceful, accepting relationships. Blues operate on an intimacy base, but seek control and being understood. Neither is completely congruent. Relationships of Blues and Whites give validity to the colloquium, "Still waters run deep."

DOER   versus   DOER
(prefers autonomy)   (prefers direction)

Whites usually get the job done. They are not particularly concerned with the timeline or exactness of their work. They do quality work and concern themselves mostly with meeting the agreement of the contract. They are steady workers who enjoy doing the job themselves as much as delegating it to others. They can be lazy and/or overwhelmed when they accept too much work at one time or lack enthusiasm for their endeavors due to rigid supervisors or unfulfilling tasks.

Blues prefer doing the job themselves rather then delegating it to others. They love the autonomy which comes from skilled jobs which require their particular expertise. In fact, one may well find the artisans of our society are most represented by Blues who enjoy the opportunity of creating and implementing their craft on their own. Subsequently, they are more inclined to trust themselves, while Whites can better delegate the responsibility to others.

CONTROLLING (power play)   versus   NEITHER SEEKS CONTROL
OR TO BE CONTROLLED

Blues want to know everything that is going on in their companion's life. Blue employers tend to be suspicious and keep their fingers in everyone's business. Blue parents are curious about all aspects of their child's life. One White young man (senior in high school) called his mom from work with a simple request for her expertise on the best brand of floor cleanser he should use in mopping up the floor at his job. Watch how the Blue mother extends a simple question into an involved conversation.

White son (on telephone): "Mom, what kind of floor cleaner do we use at home?"

Blue mom (on telephone): "Are you cleaning the floor?"

White: "Yes, Mom, now I have to go, but I just need the name of the best cleaner."

Blue: "Is anyone else helping you mop the floor?"

White: "No! Carl is cleaning the food trays."

Blue: "Who is Carl? I've never heard you mention him before."

White: "Mother! Just tell me the name of a good floor cleaner!"

Blue: "There is no need to get upset. I was just wondering how you were doing."

White: "I'm fine, Mom. Now could you just tell me the name of that floor cleaner, so I can get done and come home?"

Regardless of their age or relationship, Blues tend to try and control Whites. One of my favorite examples of this comes in the form of a note one Blue thirteen year old girl left for her forty-two year old White mother, just prior to the young girl's departure for a European vacation with her father.

Mom, Bye! See you July 10th. I love you. Here's a list *I would like* you or Randy to do.

1. Take Rover (dog) for a run *at least* every day.

2. Feed her at night.

3. Feed the fish a couple times a week.

4. Please trim the trees in front and back yard.

Thanks. Please do these for me. Especially the first two because she'll tear up the yard if you don't. Thanks again. It would make me very happy. Bye. I love you.

LOVE, MICHELLE

P.S. Oh, and Mom, please don't dust the hallway floor. (Just kidding!)

P.S.S. I'll write, don't worry.

(Personally, I don't think her mother has any need to worry. This young thirteen year old will worry enough for them both and then some.)

Another illuminating example reflecting this control issue comes when a White dentist arrives home after a long day at the office. He is greeted with a warm kiss from his Blue interior designer wife, who has just taken a phone message and promised that her husband would call right back when he arrives home.

His initial response is "Thanks for the message. I'll call back in about half an hour." "Half an hour!" she replies. "I promised her you would call her immediately."

Three more times she hammers him while he tries to digest some of the evening paper. Finally she threatens him, "Bill, either you call her right now or I'll just have to call her back and explain how you and I just don't see friendship and keeping promises the same way. After all, she is your friend and I did promise that you would call." Quietly, he hands her the phone which infuriates her more. She calls and says, "Louise, I'm terribly sorry to have to call you, but I felt you should know I've given Bill your message and he will return it when he is good and ready." And he did. About half an hour later.

Both personalities are controlling, but Blues are more likely to overly control others while Whites seek primarily to only control themselves.

EMOTIONAL   versus   EMOTIONAL AND LOGICAL

This represents a strong difference between the Blues and Whites. Blues thrive on emotional interaction. They focus on feelings (rational *and* irrational). Whites are able to work comfortably with both logical and emotional interaction. They focus on logical reasoning.

One couple (White wife, Blue husband) recently divorced and she remarked, "I could probably learn to love him again, but I can't take his excessive emotional behavior. Everything is emotional to him. I thought I had a problem our whole married life until I found out lots of people don't like to constantly deal with feelings. Actually, I was quite relieved to know I was just as normal as he was. I'm seeking a Red personality for my next relationship. I know how difficult they can be, but at least we can move from one issue to another without continually rehashing every negative thing I've ever done to him for the past twenty years."

IRRATIONAL (unrealistic   versus   IRRATIONAL (timid and
expectations)   fearful)

Blues want everyone to read their minds. They expect everyone to just *know* how they are feeling. They often say, "If I have to tell you, you don't really care." Unfortunately, that irrational thinking nonsense creates painful relationships for everyone involved with Blues. Typically Whites feel guilty when they are unable to decipher the Blues non-verbal clues on how to behave and what questions are most appropriate to ask.

Blues fantasize a lot about how things *should* be and then expect others to share the same fantasy and act accordingly. Whites come close to daydreaming like the Blues, but their fantasies generally pursue excitement and power rather than intimate relationships. Blues simply can't understand how any other path would be as interesting or important to pursue as relationships. One White male said, "She expects me to read her mind because she spends every waking minute reading mine. She tiptoes around the house every morning getting ready for work because she knows *she* would appreciate the quiet. Who cares?! Certainly not me. I'm half deaf and never would have cared what kind of racket she made over the past ten years while she quietly moved in and out of the bedroom."

Whites error with irrational behavior derived from fear and timidity. Whites often carry irrational perceptions of others and what they are *certain* will happen if they confront someone or make a wrong decision. Some Whites become almost paralyzed in their inability to risk because they somehow think they *know* what will happen. Healthy Whites readily acknowledge that they wasted many years being bashful or lonely because they "perceived" and "projected" problems which had not the least bit of rational explanation. Some White mothers are scared to death they may physically abuse their children when no evidence or history of child abuse exists. White men often refuse to date because "women will reject them" and yet they have never been rejected when asking for a date. It does become rather ridiculous to continue pursuing such irrational thinking, particularly when there is no historical or circumstantial evidence to support the perceived fear. Blue-White relationships must work to not promote each other's irrational thinking.

ACHIEVER   versus   BALANCED

Blues are more inclined to stretch themselves in life towards increased productivity, while Whites are more content balancing their lives with work and play. One couple (Blue wife, White husband) found a successful solution with him sailing many weekends with friends while she corrected papers, designed lesson plans and created new incentives for learning with her kindergarten class. She loved being well prepared for her students and he loved developing his sailing expertise and friendships.

Blues are more determined to put in whatever time and effort is required to be the best. Whites are more concerned with enjoying the total process of living which includes a balanced support system of friends, family, self and work. They are willing to sacrifice perfection and high achievement in order to have it all. However, they are vulnerable to pleasing others. On occasion, you find Whites working longer hours at the office in order to please the boss, until they are chastized by their spouses for not attending to home duties (i.e., children, the yard or other household responsibilities). Then they frantically try and please their spouse, only to be once again drawn into longer hours on the job in order to meet the boss' demands. They are known to feel terribly torn between the components of their balanced lives with high frustration of being unable to satisfy anyone including themselves.

Blues seem most content with their direction of high achievement. They value their choice of commitment enough to ignore outside influences on their priorities. One Blue woman returned from a slow-paced camping experience somewhat displeased with how bored she found herself. "There was absolutely nothing to do. I finished my five books the first two days and looked blankly at the remaining five days with rather frustrated eyes. But my husband (White personality) and our daughter had the time of their lives hiking up trails and making new friends." She never suggested or even seemed to consider that her priorities might be somewhat limited to high achievement. She simply felt the environment wasn't conducive to her needs.

INTENSE   versus   RELAXED

"I know it isn't right, but I simply can't face my children another moment after we finally get dinner over with and the dishes washed. My (White) husband rescues me by always putting the children to bed. He reads a story and says their prayers with them and I sit quietly in my room listening to them ask daddy why mommy doesn't want to read the story too. It kills me, but I really can't take them for one more minute." So goes the common complaint of involved, Blue parents. They are so intense that they can easily overwhelm themselves with relationships and have to remove themselves for a while to gather their composure.

Whites seem to roll with life's twists and turns without often losing their perspective. Much of their success lies in their ability to exercise logical as well as emotional control. They are also less involved and thus, less intense than their Blue companions. Blues appreciate Whites who get involved and share the burdens. When Whites take a more assertive position, Blues tend to calm down.

IMPATIENT   versus   PATIENT

Is it the perfectionism of the Blues that drives them to be so impatient? Is it their dominant personality? Blues tend to play the more patient role in Red-Blue relationships. However, in White-Blue relationships they generally become the more impatient of the two. They appear driven to assume the leadership role and make things happen.

Whites are typically the most patient of all the personalities. "What difference will a few minutes make?" they say. Blues are usually prompt and expect the same of others. Whites do not give "Father Time" the power Blues do. They are not as concerned with punctuality or the distress which comes with being punctual. Whites are rarely irritated with the late arrivals of family, colleagues or friends. They see little value in getting all worked up over something you really can't change anyway.

CRITICAL OF SELF   versus   TOLERANT OF OTHERS
   AND OTHERS

Two girlfriends were vacationing in Mexico when the White friend had her wallet stolen out of her purse while riding on a city bus. "I felt something tugging at my purse but never dreamed that someone would steal from me," she commented after learning that all their money and passports had been stolen. "We can replace the money, and I'm sure our passports will show up. After all, what would anyone want with them. Let's just drop by the American Embassy and explain our situation to the authorities. Everything will be fine." Her Blue friend remembered looking at her in utter amazement. "Vickie, we have just lost all our money and passports. We are in a country where the national past time is *not* baseball and they don't speak English. We have no transportation and we have *no* idea where the American Embassy is located. And you are telling me everything will be fine!!! Tell me, my friend, do you think it is possible that they took anything else with our money and identification like, for example, your mind?!" All criticism aside, they did locate the embassy and had a delightful vacation. The Blue friend, however, remained terribly suspicious of all Mexicans for the rest of the trip, while the White friend repeatedly invited the local people to join them for dinner and teach them their cultural ways.

Blue parents tend to notice the one "C" on the report card while the White parents compliment their children for attending class. Blue employees often notice their boss' lack of appreciation for all their hard work, while Whites accept that the boss deserves longer lunches because he is the boss. Generally speaking, Whites tolerate what Blues critique.

| UNFORGIVING | versus | FORGIVING, |
| AND RESENTS | | BUT REMEMBERS |

For Blues, getting mad is usually not enough. They want to get even. They will often hold the grudge as long as they feel the other person needs to be punished. One Blue wife came to see me at sixty-five years of age prepared to leave her White husband because she perceived him as "cruel and unattentive." She revealed that he had missed their daughter's sixteenth birthday *and* high school graduation. He, of course, could neither remember attending or missing either. The irony, however, lay in the reality that the daughter saw her father as more loving and supportive than her mother and held absolutely no resentment towards her father for anything. The Blue mother had made herself miserable for years over an issue that had been long forgotten by the principle parties involved.

Whites are willing to forgive, but only after they have avenged any wrong doing. Due to their quiet, slow-paced lifestyle, avenging others can take a considerable amount of time. One young White swimmer was verbally thrashed by her Red coach in front of all the other girls at an important swim meet. She said nothing to her coach. She simply listened. The final event of the meet was her best stroke. The score was tied. She could win or lose the event for her team. She led the other swimmers all the way to the finish. With a comfortable lead and only yards from touching the wall for a win, she suddenly stopped and stood up, disqualifying her in the event. Her Red coach was livid. She simply looked up at him with a contented smile, which seemed to say, "Gotcha!" After that, she continued to swim for the team. Neither continued the grudge. The "wrong" had been "righted" and all could now be forgiven and forgotten. Blue-White relationships are noted for holding resentments far longer than is healthy. They are also seen as most loving and genuine with their feelings once sincere forgiveness is sought. (Preferably on hands and knees!)

| WILLING TO DEAL WITH | versus | AVOIDS CONFLICT |
| CONFLICT ON PRINCIPLE | | |

While it is true that Blues usually assume the leadership role in Blue-White relationships, they are not particularly intrigued with conflict. Blues are the moral guardians of society and will rise to the occasion when they feel an injustice has occurred. They are often highly principled people who will not tolerate passive acceptance of "wrong" behavior. They will speak their minds and confront anyone when a situation flies in the face of truth and honesty. They are equally verbal when they feel they have been dealt with unjustly. Blues are known to act like a cornered tiger, lashing out irrationally at someone who they feel had perhaps erred in judgment or crossed them in some unforgivable way. In other words, when a Blue deems another's behavior to be unacceptable, verbal confrontation will generally take place.

Whites are less inclined to create "a scene" and stir up trouble for themselves. On one occasion, a White mother observed her young daughter being verbally abused by a cruel old man. At the time, she gave no indication that she was terribly disturbed. She did pull a face at the old man behind his back. She also brought the incident up to several other people two weeks later. However, she avoided conflict at the time of her displeasure. Whites do everyone a disservice with their attitudes that most things do not deserve at least a response.

In order to avoid conflict, Whites are notorious for constantly giving the response, "I don't care." One Blue woman remarked about her White husband, "I get so sick and tired of his 'I don't care' responses that it makes me furious whenever I hear it now. He really doesn't care whether the question concerns seeing a movie, going to dinner for the evening or even whether to get pregnant and have more children. All he ever says is, 'Whatever you would like to do is okay with me.'"

One day she was so frustrated with his answers that she asked him if they could blow their entire savings and go to Europe. As expected he, half-listening, replied that he didn't care. She purchased the tickets the next day. They went to Europe and now he appears to be somewhat more attentive and willing to express an opinion regardless of the conflict it might create for them to resolve.

COMPLIANT...TACTFUL...BEHAVED...OBLIGING

Blues and Whites share all four of these traits. They appreciate and value each other for their willingness to extend the small courtesies and appropriate manners which Reds and Yellows struggle to understand or extend to others.

These shared values help cement a warm and sincere relationship for Blue-White connections.

GIVES ADVICE AND	versus	GIVES ADVICE ONLY
EXPECTS COMPLIANCE		WHEN ASKED

Blues tend to make stronger disciplinarians than Whites. Blues feel they have a great deal to offer and willingly share it with others. When they give advice, they expect others to comply.

Whites are more inclined to allow others to set their own boundaries. They are not prone to follow up their advice in order to insure its application. They do not often give suggestions without some prodding by those seeking their advice. They may think a problem through and never verbally share their thoughts unless others specifically request their advice.

FEEL A LOT OF GUILT

Another "kindred trait" Blues and Whites share is guilt. Actually, I think they have a corner on the market. Both are uncomfortable seeing anyone hurting, regardless of the reason for the pain. Both blame themselves for their inappropriate behavior and hold onto past regrets too long. They are both capable of becoming immobile if their guilt is particularly serious. I worked with a Blue-White couple who had been separated for years, but unable to file divorce papers due to a heavy guilt for the absolution of the marriage. Neither could dissolve the marital pact because of their obligations to the children and each other. Yet, neither was willing to re-engage the relationship because of the past emotional scars and dismal potential for future success.

CARING LISTENER	versus	EXCELLENT LISTENER

I think the major difference in the listening skills between Blues and Whites is their emotional attachment to the conversation. Both care about people but Whites are more apt to objectively hear the issues, while Blues are instinctively drawn to the individual. Both are capable of giving their full attention to a discussion and responding with sincere concern for the individual and the content.

| COMPLEX DEEP WHEN SHARING FEELINGS | versus | EASY TO TALK TO; HARD TO GET FEELINGS FROM |

Blues run very deep with their emotions. They are sincere and genuine when they share themselves with others. They are often insulted when others do not fully understand their complexity and concerns. They are typically left frustrated with a conversation which lacks sufficient time for completion. They are always concerned with the emotional content of the dialogue.

Whites are quite easy to talk to. They typically don't display much emotion. They are prone to sit quietly and listen to others. They are not likely to open up unless they are certain of the other's trustworthiness. They do not handle rejection well and feel more comfortable holding their feelings inside. Many people find Whites desirable conversationalists because they would rather listen than talk. Blues and Whites are known for their sensitivity to others and appreciate the increased warmth this specifically offers them in Blue-White relationships.

| LOVES DEEPLY AND HAS STRONG COMMITMENT | versus | LOVES EASILY AND HAS STRONG COMMITMENT |

Both Blues and Whites are capable of being highly committed to each other. They value security and typically find committed relationships to be the most natural way to enjoy life. They are often traumatized with the break up of relationships with each other and neither recovers easily regardless of who terminates the relationship.

Blues are inclined to feel a deep emotional commitment with people, while Whites find it easy to accept and love those they meet. Blues are known for their "lifelong" guarantees on their love. While scars may develop within the relationship, Blues tend to feel a strong loyalty to those select few with whom they emotionally accept and commit. This invitation does not come easily for the Blues but the reward is a deep caring which often lasts the span of a lifetime.

Whites are tolerant and accepting of others. Whites commit quietly to relationships. They feel the closest to those Blues who are gentle and kind.

Blue-White relationships are generally characterized by sincerity, stability and quiet persuasion. Both colors tend to accept each other and yet, seek to promote positive changes in the relationship. Unlike most other combinations, Blue-White relationships tend to be gentle in their communication. They represent a most complementary sharing of similar values. They are also fortunate to experience unique differences from each color which broadens their capacity to successfully encounter each other and life itself.

MAKING THE MOST OF COMPLEMENTARY SIMILARITIES

BLUES NEED WHITES:	WHITES NEED BLUES:
To show them the good in others	To motivate them
To teach relaxed attitudes	To be kind to them
To listen to them	To not make them feel guilty
To respect them	To teach them creativity
To appreciate them	To encourage and believe in them
To calm their nerves	To direct them
To minimize their imperfections	To build self-confidence
To carry out specific assignments	To nurture them
To be agreeable	To initiate activities
To be emotionally responsible	To accept them as they are

POTENTIAL CONFLICTS OF
COMPLIMENTARY SIMILARITIES

BLUES	WHITES
Seek intimacy	Has difficulty expressing feelings
Committed	Uncommitted
Judgmental	Tolerant
Perfectionistic tendencies	Overwhelmed
Directed	Lazy
Passionate	Doubting
Detail conscious	Unaware
Craves verbal communication	Comfortable with non-verbal communication
Unforgiving	Unforgiving
Irrational when angered	Non-communicative when angered

Hand-in-Glove

BLUE-YELLOW RELATIONSHIPS

Blue-Yellow relationships are the most intimate combination of different color personalities. They represent the entire spectrum of emotions and, together, they can experience explosive synergy. Blue-Yellow combinations are primarily concerned with quality relationships (genuine human connectedness). Blues most commonly represent the depth, sincerity and compassion of intimacy while Yellows display the excitement, warmth and eternal optimism of relationships.

Blues and Yellows tend to value each other but often experience difficulty accepting each other's vastly different perceptions of how life is best lived. For example, Blues believe that play comes after the work is done. Yellows regard work as a necessary prerequisite in order to play but regard play as far more valuable and tend to give it first priority.

Blues are very stable while Yellows find themselves rather flighty. Blues prefer stability and Yellows seek change. Once again, the theory of "attracting opposites" appears quite accurate when we look at the unconscious choices so many Blues and Yellows make to befriend each other. They are as opposite as Red-White combinations, and yet, somehow feel strongly attracted to each other. Perhaps each fulfills what the other needs. Perhaps their differences afford them the opportunity of appreciating each other's strengths. Regardless of the reasons, Blues and Yellows frequently seek and enjoy each other's companionship. Theirs is a strong bonding of the heart.

OVERVIEW

Blue Personality	Yellow Personality
MOTIVE	
Intimacy	Fun
NEEDS	
to be appreciated	intimacy
to be understood	to be praised
to be good for self (morally)	to look good to others (socially)

acceptance	approval

WANTS

security	adventure
autonomy	autonomy
to please others	to be noticed
to reveal insecurities (openly)	to hide insecurities (loosely)

BEHAVIORAL STYLE

high complexity	low complexity
heavyweight	lightweight
purposeful and serious	playful and lighthearted
perfectionism	scattered productivity
controlling in order to get security	craves freedom
responsible	irresponsible
attention to detail	what detail?
sincere	insincere
low profile	high profile
stability	change
suspicious	trusting
conscientious	innocent
emotional	emotional
illogical	logical
too sensitive	insensitive
doer	delegator/performer
creative	innovative
intense	carefree
impatient	good natured
manipulative	seeks escape
demanding	obnoxious
direct communication (with feelings)	direct communication (with facts and feelings)
unforgiving and resents	forgiving
willing to deal with conflict based on principles	avoids confrontation

strong non-verbal	strong verbal
possessive	non-possessive
tactful	tactless with humor
behaved	rebellious
gives advice and expects compliance	gives advice but unconcerned with compliance
seeks advice from knowledgeable people	welcomes advice from others
distant	inviting
critical of self and others	accepting of self and others
self-righteous	aloof
feel a lot of guilt	rarely gives or takes guilt
blames self	blames others
negative	positive
emotionally cluttered	simple
caring listener	poor listener
complex and deep when sharing feelings	easy to share feelings with
gives with strings attached	gives freely
loves deeply and has strong commitment	loves easily, but poor commitment
lies to avoid hurting others and due to embarrassment	lies to save face

INTERPERSONAL RELATIONSHIPS

(In-depth Presentation)

Blue Personality   **Yellow Personality**

INTIMACY   versus   FUN

Yellows lighten the hearts of Blues and Blues enrich the hearts of Yellows. They make a passionate team. Whether they be parent-child, friend-friend, husband-wife, or employer-employee, this combination usually experiences positive bonds of playful creativity and committed caring.

Blues are motivated by intimacy. Yellows are motivated by fun but need intimacy. Yellows are more inclined to seek intimacy than Blues are to pursue fun. Blues typically place little value on play time, preferring to focus on the more serious aspects of life.

Yellows live by the motto, "Are we having fun yet?" No other personality seeks fun like Yellows. Yellows often live to PLAY. When Yellows become pressured at work or home, energizing hobbies or short vacations replace their haggard looks with youthful vigor. Always reward a good dog with a pat on the head and a deserving Yellow with a vacation. Yellows can't understand why anyone would commit to anything that didn't include fun. They are equally confused by people who don't know how to relax on vacations. Blues have to have a purpose to relax and play, while for Yellows, relaxing and playing *is* the purpose.

Blues commit themselves most completely to activities that enrich the Blue-Yellow relationship. They will take swimming lessons if their Yellow companion likes to swim. They are inclined to prioritize being together in the relationship and schedule their various activities around enhancing intimacy within the relationship. Blue parents typically attend their children's school, sports and other social functions regardless of the inconvenience. Blue teachers often empathize with a student who is struggling with assignments. Blue spouses plan business or community obligations around birthdays and other special holidays in order to share memorable celebrations with their family. Blues feel deeply and enjoy committing to intimate relationships regardless of the numerous expectations or difficulty.

Yellows operate on a superficial level most of the time. They are capable of feeling deeply but prefer a more limited emotional connection on a daily basis. Yellows are often accused by Blues of not really caring because they appear so superficial. Equally frustrating for the Blues is the Yellows' perception that Blues are so controlling because of their committed and involved nature. Yellows often remark that the price of being loved by Blues is, at times, too high. When they "emotionally" meet at mutually satisfying levels, no other mixed color combination can match their intimacy. They are funny, casual, sincere, accepting, endearing, and vibrant in their connection.

TO BE APPRECIATED   versus   TO BE PRAISED

When a Yellow wants to learn how to get along with a Blue, it's really quite simple. The first thing they must do every morning after they wake up is tell their Blue companion, "I love you and appreciate all you do for me." As long as Yellows are sincere, they will be on "easy street" for life. Blues thrive on emotional closeness and appreciation. They willingly forego personal pleasure in order to meet other's needs. It means so much when others, however briefly, forego personal pleasure to appreciate them. The theme of Blues could easily come from the play Camelot. King Arthur so aptly suggests in one song that the way "to handle a woman, is to love her, simply love her." Nothing could be more true for Blue men and women. They simply need to know you love and appreciate them in order for life to be complete.

Blues give at such a committed level that mere praise would not generally suffice. They are typically unimpressed with social acknowledgement especially at a superficial level. Blues are more inclined to value a brief handwritten note of acknowledgement by someone who truly understands and appreciates their contribution.

On the other hand, Yellows typically throw things together at the last minute and come up smelling like a rose. Appreciation is generally unnecessary for them. A congratulatory pat on the back and public acknowledgement (when appropriate) will sufficiently meet their needs.

TO BE GOOD FOR   versus   TO LOOK GOOD TO
SELF (morally)   OTHERS (socially)

Walt Disney's character, Jiminy Cricket, would call it a conscience. I call it character. Call it whatever you prefer, but in the end it means that Blues are more concerned with their moral obligations while Yellows need social recognition. I remember consulting with a Blue patient directly after a Yellow patient one day. Both patients had become drunk at their mother-in-laws' twenty-fifth wedding anniversary celebration. I was fascinated with how differently they approached their concern about their drunken behavior. The Blue patient needed to know if he should apologize for his drunken state. He was concerned that a proper son-in-law would have remained sober and helped host the party. The Yellow patient needed to know if I thought others in the family would think poorly of him. He was more concerned about tainting his social image with his in-laws than the inappropriateness of his behavior. The Blue suffered from moral guilt while the Yellow suffered from social guilt.

Another illuminating example of the difference lies in the matter of weight control. Blues need to keep in shape for reasons of self-acceptance while Yellows need to look good for others. Yellows typically operate from personal vanity while the Blues are primarily concerned with self-respect.

SECURITY   versus   PLAYFUL ADVENTURE

Blues are often envious of Yellow's self-esteem. Yellows carry their self-esteem (often from birth) within themselves. They do not seek security from outside sources. They like themselves and usually feel confident that everything will work out in the end. This confidence allows them to seek adventure throughout their lives while Blues continually grasp for the elusive feeling of security. Perhaps one reason Blues seek Yellows is the comfort they feel in connecting with someone who innately exudes confidence and security.

On the other hand, Yellows value the security they receive from Blues. Blues work very hard to foster security for those they love. Yellows intuitively sense the deep commitment that Blues offer and generally strive to keep Blues in their life. Just prior to leaving on a business trip, a Blue woman discovered that her Yellow husband had worked out a business deal behind her back with his father. She could not tolerate his father. She threatened to leave her husband because she could no longer accept his deceiving interactions with his father. This carefree, light-hearted man was heart-broken. The thought of losing his wife became an obsession. He called her every night while she was away on business to the point of harassment. He wanted reassurance that she still loved him and would stay with him. Upon her arrival home at the airport, he met her with roses and a limousine. He read a poem he had written for her. Subconsciously, Yellows may seek Blues because they value security and know that of all the personalities, Blues are not only most likely to seek security, but *offer* it as well.

Yellows love stretching themselves experientially. They curiously pursue many facets of life. They are primarily interested in playful adventure and find extreme competition unappealing. Yellows risk freely. They will change jobs, living conditions and friends more comfortably than Blues. They enjoy the thrill of trying something new and require constant challenges of a playful nature to hold their interest.

AUTONOMY   versus   FREEDOM

The words autonomy and freedom convey difference in purpose. Blues want autonomy in their pursuit of a task. Yellows want freedom *from* completing a task as well as freedom to work on their own within a work setting. In organizations, Blues and Yellows find independent work situations very comfortable. Both Blues and Yellows prefer to be given their responsibilities and allowed to perform them in their own way and time. They accept direction but resist control. Blues enjoy the creative aspect of autonomy and thrive on the possibilities of striving for perfection when no one else is able to force them to accept mediocrity. Yellows enjoy the social interaction with people, but prefer the freedom to work at their own pace without others setting deadlines and forcing unnecessary meetings. Both tend to find that teamwork often cramps their natural style and preference.

EMOTIONAL HEAVYWEIGHT versus EMOTIONAL LIGHTWEIGHT

Blues tend to remain committed to the cause of intimacy regardless of emotional scarring while Yellows are quick to seek refuge upon personal disappointments. The animal kingdom offers us two role models. Blues are similar to the dog pursuing a rabbit. He is focused and determined. He will rest at nothing to accomplish whatever he has set out to do. He is oblivious to other distractions. He tenaciously pursues his goal. Blues are predictably emotional and usually remain focused on this behavior throughout their life.

Yellows are like the butterfly, darting in and out of nature with a "look and see" attitude. They never land anywhere too long and maintain a safe distance from any undesired connection. Beautiful, gentle and exciting, they attract everyone's attention but generally give only limited exposure of themselves.

Blues are usually direct and consistent with their emotional intentions. Yellows are more vague and unpredictable. Both value sincere commitments, despite their differences in how they emotionally commit.

PURPOSEFUL AND SERIOUS	versus	PLAYFUL AND LIGHTHEARTED

YELLOW: (to wife) "Wouldn't it be fun to be in Paris this Spring? Just think of how colorful and exciting it would be."

BLUE: (to husband) "I would love the romance of Paris in Springtime. But I want to go when I know we are really in love. Just going to Europe for the sake of traveling doesn't excite me much."

Many Yellows could be nicknamed "the Yellow tease." They motion with one hand to come close and with the other hand to stay away. They are seductive with their charm and innocence but too easily frightened away. They shine like the sun and entice with their very existence, but quickly laugh it all off when the Blues in their lives become serious.

This is particularly frustrating for Blues who rarely invest themselves lightly (particularly in relationships). They find the Yellows casual attitude difficult to respect or depend on. Yellows are often baffled with the seriousness which Blues approach relationships with, considering Blues to be too concerned and over-zealous in their commitment. "All I wanted," Yellows explain while dating, "was to have some good, clean fun. The way Blues act, you'd think we were getting married or something."

STRONG PERFECTIONISM   versus   SCATTERED PRODUCTIVITY

Watching Blues go through life is like watching Chris Evert-Lloyd on the tennis court. They have penetrating concentration and notice all details. They willingly work out until they are practice-perfect. Blues value people who express the same commitment to perfection regardless of their professional field. They often enjoy the admiration of others for their devotion to perfection. In relationships, however, this proves to be particularly frustrating for both Blues and Yellows. Yellows become frustrated with the constant need of Blues to do "everything" perfectly. Yellows are sometimes less excited about actually having to *live with* "Michaelangelo," the famous Blue painter, than they are simply viewing his masterful perfection on tour of the Sistine Chapel from an intimate distance.

Yellows are more like watching Ilie Nastasie on the tennis courts. This lively Romanian player impressed tennis fans for years with his brilliant moments of tennis play and equally brilliant childish antics, which he predictably displayed to their amusement on the courts. He was clearly as interested in social approval as technical expertise.

This style of scattered productivity often proves terribly frustrating for Blues who cannot understand how anyone, let alone this person they are in love with (particularly spouse, child or parent), can skate through life with such little concern for accuracy and dedication to perfection. Blues need to understand that Yellows *will* be hostile and uncooperative, forsaking all their charismatic charm, if necessary, to insure their selfish demands for freedom. Given healthy choices, however, Yellows will generally balance playfulness with meaningful productive moments.

CONTROLLING IN ORDER   versus   SEEKS FREEDOM
    TO GET SECURITY

Blue personalities tend to prefer a conventional, deliberate and predictable relationship. They have such strong needs for stability that they try and hold everything together in order to feel peace of mind. Blues are so appropriate and exacting that they often select themselves as the leader of Blue-Yellow relationships. Yellows instinctively resist control. They refuse to give control to Blues without a price. Depending on the character of either person, this price could be extremely high.

Blues often appear controlling because they need to feel secure in the relationship and they think this security comes by always knowing what Yellows are doing, and where they are going. Blues also appear controlling because they feel it is essential that they remind Yellows about proper manners and appropriate public behavior. This behavior is typically construed by Yellows as unnecessary and demeaning.

Yellows enjoy a flexible, changing, and unstructured relationship. They reject hard boundaries (i.e., "be home for dinner every night by 6:00 p.m.") and find little need for stability. Freedom is essential to Yellows in order to experience life at its best. Yellows prize the freedom to choose who they will be with, where they will go, and how they will get there. Easily manipulated, they are quite receptive to the Blues who allow them to freely choose their options in life. Admittedly, without healthy character, Yellows do abuse their "rights to freedom" and may find themselves unable to commit to relationships, pursuing instead a more self-centered (as opposed to cooperative) lifestyle.

RESPONSIBLE   versus   IRRESPONSIBLE

"Just tell me if you hear of anyone putting on the play *The Wizard of Oz,*" one Blue mother lamented to me. "I have the perfect one to play the part of the brainless scarecrow—my son!" She was so frustrated with his irresponsible behavior. "Seriously," she continued, "it won't hurt my feelings. Just tell me straight out, is it possible that he will ever get a brain?!" Her Yellow son was quite representative of many irresponsible Yellows. Yellows rarely stop and think before they speak or act.

Yellows are more vainly concerned with their physical appearance than the fact that they live in a pig sty for a bedroom. Yellows are notorious for walking on expensive sweaters which they may or may not have paid for with their own money. Yellow teenagers seem to epitomize the Yellow irresponsibility because most teenagers already suffer universally during this exasperating transition from childhood to adulthood. Yellow babysitters are terrific at playing with the children but prefer to talk on the telephone with friends rather than clean up the messes they left having a good time with the kids.

Yellows are more concerned with the speed they turn the corner with, than the "wear and tear" on the car tires. One Blue father was always concerned with the costs his Yellow son incurred while living at home. "From sheer negligence alone," he'd say, "you have cost me more than all your brothers and sisters combined." He always encouraged his son to get a good paying job in order to financially survive in the outside world on his own.

Yellows don't give adequate consideration for the long term consequences of their behavior. They do not typically take good care of their belongings because they only think for the moment. Blues usually resist loaning camping equipment, cars, and other important equipment to Yellows. Yellows have rather irresponsible natures.

On the other hand, Blues make marvelous companions to Yellows. Like Wendy in the classic Walt Disney film, *Peter Pan,* Blues constantly work to help Yellows "grow up" and be responsible. They notice details and constantly acquaint Yellows with reasons why details (like stop signs, high school diplomas, and clothes hangers) exist.

SINCERE   versus   INSINCERE

Blues pride themselves in their sincere and loyal commitments to Yellows. One Blue client, Rob, came in and demanded an explanation of how his best friend, John, (a Yellow) could leave for a brief summer vacation and then decide to *stay* in Albuquerque, New Mexico for his coming senior year in high school rather than returning to Southern California. "We were best friends," Rob explained. "I don't think he realized how much I invested in our friendship. And now, on a whim, he just up and leaves me for the thrill of a new environment. If that is all I meant to him, we must not have had a great friendship at all." Rob was devastated to think his friend would consider abandoning him after all they had shared through two previous years of high school.

Rob and John had great times while they were together. Now John was prepared to experience something new. It had just come up as a fluke and he was game for anything. "After all," Yellows explain, "you only live once." This seems so insincere to Blues who willingly sacrifice "the thrill of it all" for their committed relationships. Yellows feel differently. They give what they've got while they are in the situation, and then comfortably move on when it changes.

LOW PROFILE   versus   HIGH PROFILE

Picture this. Two people apply for positions with a touring production company. One specifically requests a position designing and sewing costumes behind the scenes, while the other expresses a strong preference to be on stage. Which one is most likely Blue and which one do you suspect will be Yellow? The odds have it that Blues prefer the behind the scenes details, while the Yellows enjoy front stage exposure. One enjoys working with things while the other prefers people.

SUSPICIOUS   versus   TRUSTING/NAIVE

"My wife is better than the FBI," one Yellow husband explained. "She knows everything I've done wrong since the day we began dating. I would hate to see the WANTED poster she would design if I were a criminal."

"It's true," she agrees, "We just got home from a vacation in Mexico with another couple. One day, our husbands wanted to go fishing. My friend's husband threw his wife a kiss from a distance and told her to eat dinner without him because he wasn't certain what time they would return. She laughed, and barely skipped a sentence in our conversation. Not me! I demanded to inspect the boat for seaworthiness and get his lifejacket (which I purchased and packed knowing he might want to go boating). I didn't trust him, the boat or myself. Can you imagine my husband dying in a boating accident and leaving me to raise two kids by myself?"

Many Blues go through life too suspicious of others. They are rarely free to really enjoy pleasureable moments because they are so busy suspecting what may go wrong.

As much as Blues suffer from their suspicious minds, Yellows may suffer from their non-discriminating natures. Too often wonderful Yellows allow negative friends to enter their life and color it ugly. They unwittingly never believe people could have such negative motives. They naively invite inappropriate people their way because as Yellows say, "the people are fun" or "they really are good people once you get to know them inside."

Yellow innocence is caused for concern by Blue parents who value their child's refreshing enthusiasm but fear the inevitable tragedies which comes from not taking precautions. One Blue mother even sent her Yellow daughter away to a private school in order to break up a budding romance with a negative boyfriend. "Call me controlling or whatever you want," she cried. "I couldn't bear to see this perfectly charming child turn sarcastic, cold, and hardened right before my eyes."

It was a great move. No deception. Right up front, the young girl knew the reasons and, being Yellow, quickly found the exciting possibilities in being away from home and venturing out into the world "on her own." She went to the private school and quickly found herself responding positively to new friends and her changed environment and lifestyle.

TOO SENSITIVE   versus   INSENSITIVE

To a Blue, everything is personal. They feel deeply responsible for whatever happens in their life. This extreme sensitivity can make them particularly unpleasant on a daily basis. If you arrive late, Blues may feel badly, thinking you didn't really want to come. If you are angry, Blues typically feel guilty for possibly creating recent dilemmas in your life. Blues take many people and experiences too personally. Coupled with Yellows' carefree attitudes and flippant comments, Blues often struggle with the Yellows' insensitivity. Blues tend to create many of their emotional traumas with their own hypersensitivity. Their difficulties often seem further complicated by Yellows' insensitivity.

One Blue woman was frightened about an upcoming river rafting expedition. She mistakenly asked two Yellow friends, who had been river rafting, if she would enjoy the experience. They flippantly reassured her, almost mocking her fear. She was furious when they wouldn't express serious concern for her discomfort. Her friends were insensitive. She was too sensitive. Perhaps nothing short of a violin serenade and discussion of the need for increased life insurance would have made her happy. (And that would have probably depressed her.)

IMPATIENT   versus   GOOD NATURED

Blue-Yellow relationships often find these behaviors in conflict. Blues want their family home every night for dinner and Yellows want to be greeted with a smile and a kiss. Yellows want flexibility as to what time they will arrive home while Blues want understanding for why they don't always present themselves with a smile at the exact moment Yellows decide to grace the front door.

Blues struggle with the notion that they know what is best for everyone, especially Yellows. Yellows tend to forget time, people, commitments and any other unnecessary hassle which may complicate their lives. Yellows are often preferred by children because of their casual style which frustrates the Blues. They are certain that the only reason Yellows are more loved is because they don't demand anything of anybody. Blues want things done right and done immediately. Yellows want things done also, but freely give allowances when unforseen circumstances arise. (Unforseen circumstances can be anything from a friend calling to play golf to a death in the family.) Yellows believe that most things aren't worth getting upset over and let them pass without giving them much notice. Blues notice everything (especially noisy children and late office reports) and feel obligated to make them an issue.

UNFORGIVING   versus   FORGIVING

This represents, perhaps, the best strength of Yellows and the greatest liability for Blues. Yellows do not generally give energy to the past. (They have a hard enough time remembering it, let alone giving energy to it.) Blues harbor tremendous anger, resentment and bitterness over past encounters of the negative kind. They find it most difficult to let go of the feelings that Yellows rarely experience. If Yellows do feel deep anger or hostility, it seems to dissipate without much action on their part. They tend to live a much less cluttered life because of it.

One Blue patient expressed (in the same breath) how she had finally forgiven her ex-husband who left her for another woman. "I secretly hope someday to see him bald, and fat with his stomach desperately hanging over his pants and underwear hanging out in back." With all sincerity, she then asked, "But don't you think I am finally forgiving him?"

Blues must learn to forgive or they will frighten their Yellow companions away from any genuine sharing and intimacy. This, in turn, keeps Blues from experiencing their primary motivation in life—intimacy.

WILLING TO DEAL WITH   versus   AVOIDS CONFRONTATION
CONFLICT ON PRINCIPLES

There are certain issues which Blues do not consider negotiable. They are willing to lay their reputations on the line for these issues. They will fight like a mother bear protecting a new born cub rather than acquiesce in the name of peace. Blue spouses often find themselves angered by Yellows who won't "prove their love" by engaging in a good, wholesome argument. Blues feel honest expression of feelings shows that one cares. Blues are more inclined to suffer the consequences of a stressed relationship in order to make themselves clearly understood on important principles.

Yellows are more inclined to avoid the inevitable confrontation by laughing it off or quickly refocusing the conversation to a less controversial subject. Yellows are often seen as disloyal or "talking out of both sides of their mouth" because of their unwillingness to take a firm stand on issues. Yellows are, perhaps, too easily persuaded to abandon a particular philosophy or principle because it requires too much effort.

DISTANT   versus   INVITING

For many reasons, Blues are more intimidating than the Yellows. Yellows have a winning way about them which invites people into their lives. "Everywhere I go, I meet the nicest people," one Yellow patient remarked. Life is much like a mirror and subsequently Yellows seem to find invitations waiting for them wherever they go. Yellows warm up to people regardless of their age, race or socio-economic level.

Blues are more discriminating and judgmental. They are reserved and suspicious from a distance. They are most often only loved after a substantial "getting to know them" period of time. For the Blues, their motto remains, "to *know* me is to love me." Yellows, are just the opposite—"to *love* me is to know me." Once Yellows feel invited into someone's heart, they willingly become vulnerable and expressive.

BLAMES SELF   versus   BLAMES OTHERS

Blues typically look inward to interpret poor relationships, while Yellows, fearing the rejection created by owning up to their limitations, usually look elsewhere for places to put the blame. This often keeps Yellows from properly developing themselves. If they are not careful, Yellows can spend a lifetime explaining away their failures by placing responsibility on a multitude of sources. Only when they can look within, and see the importance of responding to their limitations, will Yellows ever know the real power which comes from accepting responsibility for oneself.

One Yellow child repeatedly blamed his problems of school truancy, sexual identity crisis, and auto theft on his "controlling and demanding" Blue father. He actually seemed to enjoy watching his poor father agonize over what he had done to his son, and how he "should" have done things differently. It took this Yellow child four years of frustration and personal disappointments before he ever began to see his part in the relationship. Eventually he claimed some responsibility and began developing more appropriate living skills.

NEGATIVE   versus   POSITIVE

Blues seem to zero in on why something can't be done while Yellows immediately see the reasons why it ought to be tried. Blues ask: "Why me? Couldn't it happen to someone else instead?!" Yellows ask: "Why not me? I think I'd be the perfect choice!" Blues tend to see all the problems while Yellows typically see all the possibilities.

CARING LISTENER   versus   POOR LISTENER

Yellows are usually out for a good time and that rarely includes sincere listening. They are not interested in emotional details and often find sitting and sharing serious concerns of others to be quite boring. Blues enjoy the idea of deep sharing and genuinely care about what the other person is trying to say. They are excellent at really listening rather than concentrating on what *their* comments will be.

Blues can be very disappointed in Yellow's superficial style of listening. They may even feel betrayed in a conversation where Yellows only hear words and neglect to focus on the feelings.

Yellows are typically frustrated with the storytelling of Blues. Blues tend to overkill their communication by relating every detail several times. You've heard, no doubt, the phrase "To make a long story short..." Blues prefer the other version, "To make a short story longer..." Blues simply want to be understood and tend to keep talking with the subconscious hope that they will be eventually understood.

GIVES WITH STRINGS   versus   GIVES FREELY
ATTACHED

Blues are typically more inclined to give of themselves than Yellows. However, when Yellows give, they give freely without expectation, while Blues often have strings attached. Many Blue personalities become angered at the "shabby" way they are treated after bending over backwards for others. Numerous individuals have shared resentments with me about guests who have stayed in their home and been treated like kings and queens without even a word of appreciation. Yellows rarely feel the same depth of disappointment. Either they simply give less or when they *do* give, Yellows don't combine the gift with any expectations.

LOVES DEEPLY AND HAS   versus   LOVES EASILY, BUT
STRONG COMMITMENT   POOR COMMITMENT

Blues have a strong loyalty to whomever and whatever they commit. They are most comfortable in committed relationships and feel great apprehension in abandoning any commitments they make. One Blue colleague of mine experienced deep emotional turmoil while trying to decide whether to stay with her husband who offered her good fun but no emotional depth, or leave her marriage for a man she had loved deeply as a friend for years. In the end there was no real decision. She loved her husband and could never leave him regardless of the empty moments she endured.

In contrast, I remember heading for the ski slopes one time with a Yellow friend. He reminded me a great deal of Peter Pan with his incessant acts of irresponsibility and refusal to accept society's demands that he grow up. He claimed that he felt too restricted, confined and committed in marriage. He wanted to play more than he wanted the responsibility of a wife and the children he had fathered.

Within a year of our conversation, my friend had abandoned his wife and two children for a more playful lifestyle. Yellows tend to be more vulnerable in the long run because they lack the depth of commitment which is required in order to experience earned intimacy.

This exciting combination of opposites offers the possibilities that neither personality could experience on their own. They share a mutual admiration. Yellows prize Blues for their talent, creativity, sensitivity, loyalty, commitment, sincerity and intimacy. Blues value Yellows for their vigor, optimism, acceptance, forgiveness, spice, candor and intimacy. Both relish the Blue-Yellow relationship's strong intimate potential and usually recognize the unique synergy afforded them together.

MAKING THE MOST OF COMPLEMENTARY OPPOSITES

BLUES NEED YELLOWS:	YELLOWS NEED BLUES:
To keep a healthy "here and now" perspective	To give grounding and direction
To promote creative, playful moments	To teach compassion and sensitivity
To foster optimism and hope	To notice details and specifics
To cherish and appreciate them	To provide stability
To remind them of their intrinsic value	To encourage the completion of tasks
To make them laugh	To remember important events and facts
To keep conversations flowing	To laugh at them
To facilitate social relationships	To praise and notice them
To promote simplicity	To provide moral leadership
To share intimate moments with	
To show them the lighter side of life	

POTENTIAL CONFLICTS OF COMPLEMENTARY OPPOSITES

BLUES	YELLOWS
Very committed	Often flighty
Too sensitive	Often sarcastic (teasing)
Generally work-oriented	Prefers playful activity
Controlling	Obsessed with freedom
Detail-oriented	Lackadaisical
Serious orientation	Lighthearted and carefree
Take on too many responsibilities	Too irresponsible
Acts appropriate and proper	Often inappropriate and ill mannered
Too selfless	Too self-obsessed
Requires long deliberation in decision making	Makes decisions spontaneously

CHAPTER TWELVE

The White and Yellow Connections

Peace and Tolerance

WHITE-WHITE RELATIONSHIPS

White-White relationships are readily identified by their peaceful existence. White-White combinations are relaxed and patient. They do not expend excess energy on trivial power struggles or concern with details. This combination tolerates each other's differences. They are both more comfortable ignoring irritable behaviors than making them an issue. Subsequently, what often creates serious conflict for other personality combinations hardly makes an impact on the White-White connection.

Whites are not usually drawn to leadership. White-White combinations struggle without clearly defined leadership roles. Both typically wait for the other to take the lead. Whites are mutually comfortable living as relaxed and unstructured companions. Neither is driven to plan or make strong goals for the future. Neither is upset if one decides to plan something or commit the other to a future goal.

White-White combinations share a high tolerance for each other and the world around them. They are very flexible and accommodating. They allow for each other's independent preferences (i.e., personal hobbies or work schedules) and dependence (i.e., listening to each other's concerns for hours). This personality combination understands the importance of a "safe port in the storm of life" and offer that gift in friendship, family or career relationships.

While White-White color combinations are not commonly represented in marital relationships, they represent a very agreeable combination in friendship. Marriage poses leadership role concerns. Friendship does not. As long as the relationship is well structured and firmly established, this combination has little difficulty successfully operating under established guidelines and expectations. The two elements this combination primarily struggles with are *motivation* and *leadership*. Charactered Whites work very hard to develop self-motivation techniques and assertion skills. With these acquired skills in place, White-White combinations are more likely to succeed in whatever role and relationship they may experience.

PEACE

Whites get along with each other. They are both motivated by peace. Each brings the necessary tolerance and patience to relationships in order to insure peace. This is clearly an example of "getting what you give." An interesting illustration of this strong motivation in all Whites comes with a look at world geography. White nations (i.e., Switzerland or Finland) are very peace loving and rarely, if ever, start wars. They are, however, known to maintain a strong defense when attacked by other, more aggressive, nations. White companionships are similar in their behavior to White nations. They strive for peaceful coexistence whenever possible. They are, however, quick to defend themselves when outside forces interfere with their relationship.

PATIENT AND TOLERANT

This combination is very slow to anger or prejudice. They are quiet in their accepting ways. They do not demand that other colors be as patient or tolerant. They simply role model their value system in a consistent and unabrasive manner. White-White connections remind us of the lives of Mahatma Ghandi or Martin Luther King. Both men quietly challenged an angry world of prejudice and injustice without need for great fanfare or publicity. White-White relationships are unobtrusive. They live simply and allow others to simply live.

SATISFIED

Imagine a relationship that does not foster unnecessary disagreement or dwell on serious conflict. Imagine White on White. These friendships rarely complain of having difficulty getting along with each other. They do not dwell on minor disappointments. In fact, they rarely even notice the problems until other colors point them out. This combination is the least willing to expend energy on negative conflict. They are the satisfied ones.

UNPRODUCTIVE COMPLACENCY

Being unaware of other's faults is a blessing. Being unaware of one's circumstances is irresponsible. Many White-White combinations allow themselves to become very complacent in their relationship and ignore the circumstances that surround them. They are like the unconcerned high school students who drop out early without graduating and suddenly find themselves undesirable in the working world. White-White combinations often remain oblivious to changing environmental circumstances and end up on the short end of the stick. When push comes to shove, this combination is often too passive and unproductive. They tend to prefer the easier path which may leave them unaware and vulnerable to a more assertive and changing environment.

This combination is notorious for leaving things that should be done today until tomorrow. They procrastinate and, without someone who is more determined, they are likely to put off important responsibilities. They tolerate each other's relaxed ways. To the extreme, this could result in a most unproductive lifestyle. Hawaii, as a state, experienced the trauma many White-White couple do. They remained complacent in their garden paradise until they suddenly awakened to the realization that outside investors were buying their land right out from under them, leaving them with nothing to eventually pass on to their grandchildren. White-White connections can remain so unproductive and complacent that they become victims of other, more determined color combinations. They must learn to balance their relaxed and complacent preferential lifestyle with assertive productivity in order to successfully endure the ever-changing demands of daily living.

SELF-DOUBTING AND INDECISIVE

This combination suffers most from self-doubt. They are often second-guessing themselves on past decisions and personal capabilities. They tend to foster each other's self-doubt because neither is usually convinced that they have made the best choices. Both are more prone to asking questions about each other's decisions than taking a direct position in support or opposition of whatever decision was made. Each waits for the other to react in order to determine whether they were right or wrong. Often neither gives a strong reaction, so the questions of one's decision-making skills remain unanswered. Self-confidence comes from within oneself. Confidence comes from doing. Neither risking or accepting oneself are strengths of Whites and, subsequently, self-doubt and indecision often remain stumbling blocks in a relationship exclusively comprised of them.

RELUCTANT, TIMID, UNINVOLVED

Whites can be boring or appear to be boring because of their reluctant, timid and uninvolved nature. White-White combinations can comfortably do nothing for a long period of time, yet drive everyone else around them into a frenzy.

One White-White couple dated for years before getting married. Their courtship consisted primarily of joint television watching and sleep. They would often call each other late at night on the telephone and one or both would fall asleep during the conversation. Not to worry! They were terribly patient with each other. They fell out of love shortly after marriage. They lived together five more years before terminating the relationship. After all, *who* would file the divorce papers?! Both were reluctant to make the first move. Neither was that involved in other relationships to necessitate divorce, and so their marriage remained, at least on the legal books, until outside friends finally pushed the woman to pull the plug. Forcing issues in life can be traumatic to a White-White relationship. Unfortunately, their timidity often promotes an unhealthy compromise between this color combination rather than stretching both parties to take a more responsible position in problem resolution.

White-White relationships seek a peaceful coexistence. They prefer to float over life's hassles rather than directly face them. They are patient and tolerant with each other and their world. They remain gentle and satisfied observers of life. They remain vulnerable to outside influences. This combination timidly avoids risks and having to make decisions. They prefer a quiet, secure and unobstrusive existence to a flashy, dynamic and demanding lifestyle. Reflective of the water they represent they flow deeply and evenly throughout their shared life experience.

Gentle Fun

WHITE-YELLOW RELATIONSHIPS

This relationship is about the "nice guys" or "good old boys (girls)." They are affable individuals, seeking an easy (as opposed to difficult) style of interaction and limited expectations. Neither chooses to hassle the other. Neither is particularly keen about directing the other either. They can be excellent friends, colleagues or parent-child, but rarely find themselves in a committed, intimate relationship. Almost as if there is no magnetism, they instinctively recognize the limitations of their companionship in surviving the rigors of daily living.

I was engaged twice to a wonderful, gentle, delightful girl but could never "sign the dotted line." I realize now that while there was a strong physical chemistry and an emotional comfortability, our relationship felt incomplete. I am Yellow and she is White. I needed someone stronger and bolder at the time to win a commitment from me. Having developed my character over the years, I am certain we could successfully complete the puzzle because I've added new pieces that were not there in my innate personality.

Whites and Yellows accommodate each other. They do not generally motivate each other. Perhaps they lack the feracity or drive Reds and Blues innately have to "light each other's fires." As children, similar values and preferances for playful activity invite a natural blend. As friends in adolenence and early adulthood, their gentle natures prarde a positive connection. As charactered adults, they appreciate each other's accepting and easy style. Theirs is a casual blending of two comfortably independent lifestyles.

OVERVIEW

White Personality	Yellow Personality
MOTIVE	
Peace	Fun
NEEDS	
power & control of self	intimacy
to be respected	to be praised
to feel good within self	to look good to others (socially)

acceptance	approval

WANTS

secure excitement	playful adventure
protection	freedom
to please self & others	to be noticed
to reveal insecurities	to hide insecurities (loosely)

BEHAVIOR STYLE

stability	change
low profile	high profile
neither seeks control or to be controlled	craves freedom
boring	exciting
passive	active
reluctant	engaging
loner	involving
tenacious	easily distracted
plow horse	race horse
feels deeply, finds expression of feelings difficult	emotional and expressive
logical & emotional	logical & emotional
direct communication	direct communication
(with feelings & facts)	(with feelings and facts)
doer	delegator/performer
likes backstage	likes front stage
patient	good-natured
non-demanding	obnoxious
relaxed	carefree
non-possessive (unless threatened)	non-possessive
craves peace	avoids confrontation
strong non-verbal	strong verbal
quiet manipulation	seeks escape
loves easily & strong commitment	loves easily, but poor commitment
consistent producer	scattered productivity & playfulness

compliant with rules	defiant of rules
tactful	tactless (with humor)
gives advice only when asked	gives advice but unconcerned with compliance
seeks advice freely	welcomes positive advice from others
intimidated	inviting
tolerant of others	accepting of others
feels inadequate	aloof
feels a lot of guilt	rarely gives or takes guilt
lies to avoid conflicts & repercussions	lies to save face and to keep from disappointing others
forgiving but remembers	forgiving

INTERPERSONAL RELATIONSHIPS

(In-depth Presentation)

White Personality   **Yellow Personality**

PEACE   versus   FUN

Whites can't understand why Yellows must go to all the trouble they do in developing relationships, meeting personal commitments (i.e., mostly playful activity) and over-extending themselves in community, school or work. Whites are more inclined to go with the flow and typically become frustrated when their Yellow friends over commit and/or try to drag them into all their "unnecessary" commitments. "If I had known life with you would have been this hectic," one White woman exclaimed to her busy Yellow roommate, "I would have taken fewer classes and hired on as your personal secretary. This is absolute madness, with the whole world constantly calling us and men always tramping through our house. Do you suppose we could start charging rent or at least retain an answering service?" Whites remind me of the "good old boys" from the South, trying very hard to uncomplicate their lives while Yellows keep committing, connecting and conversing in order to make life fun.

Whites are more interested in getting along with others than having the last laugh. Whites quietly accept many of the Yellow's limitations, while Yellows tend to verbally tease Whites and poke fun at their limitations.

POWER AND CONTROL   versus   INTIMACY
OF SELF

Whites are concerned with developing a safe environment, while Yellows risk more freely for an intimate relationship. Yellows are more interactive and their White companions remain more reserved. Whites are like cats, able to come and go autonomously and comfortably on their own. Yellows are like dogs, always seeking to be noticed, petted and played with by their companions.

TO BE RESPECTED   versus   TO BE PRAISED

Whites need to have their wishes respected. They resent being pushed into decisions which they find uncomfortable. Whites appear (behaviorally) to need constant praise and attention. In reality, they have little need of appreciation for either. They want you to respect their pace in life and preferences. Since Whites are not a verbal group, they resent having to always speak up in order to secure their right to be left alone, be with certain friends, or whatever else they deem desirable. Yellows could generally care less about respect. They want to be noticed and praised. They become so frustrated with their White friends who don't talk, but rather, simply expect Yellows to know their desires and respect them. Perhaps one of the most difficult interactions for the White-Yellow combination is their differing need for respect and praise. Whites are not known for their skill or interest in the praising of others. Yellows are often disrespectful of others and typically overstep their acceptable boundaries with Whites.

PROTECTION   versus   FREEDOM

Yellows tend to be more confident than Whites. Yellows risk more freely and, therefore, seem more comfortable with the unknown, while Whites prefer safer surroundings. Yellows often challenge their White friends to reach out and try "wild and crazy" experiences. Whites are more concerned with how they will be after trying the "wild and crazy" experiences. Yellows are more inclined to leave Whites hanging "emotionally" while they recklessly bound through life. Whites want more commitment in knowing they are secure and safe in the relationship.

STABILITY   versus   CHANGE

Whites and Yellows do not often see life through the same pair of glasses. Whites want to see the same scene and Yellows keep changing the picture. Whites appreciate the many opportunities Yellows bring to them in life but don't find it necessary to experience it all so rapidly or inconveniently. Yellows thrive on the fast pace and seldom feel inconvenienced as long as they're having a good time.

BORING   versus   EXCITING

If either has the inclination to fall in a rut, it's the Whites. Whites are often plagued by the *"sameness syndrome"*—same car, same books, same friends, same house. Yellows struggle with the exact opposite—the *"differentness syndrome."* Everything in their life is in a constant state of flux. They are always trying new foods, traveling to new places, meeting new friends and buying new cars. Both can be quite beneficial to each other when they allow their differences to provide a positive balance. On the negative end, both can feel constantly harassed by the other's lifestyle.

RELUCTANT   versus   ENGAGING

Whites are reluctant to pursue uncomfortable situations. They often need coaxing from their Yellow friends to try new experiences. Yellows willingly involve Whites in their activities. Yellows are so engaging and non-demanding that Whites find them difficult to resist. If anything, Yellows get tired of having to convince Whites to stretch and risk a little more.

TENACIOUS   versus   EASILY DISTRACTED

Whites are similar to the plow horse in the field. They are consistent and tenacious in their efforts to complete a task. They allow very little to deter them once they are committed to a cause. Yellows are more easily deterred from committing over any length of time to relationships or activities. They float like butterflies, staying briefly in one place before darting off to a more appealing location. Whites can become frustrated with the flippant, unreliable nature of Yellows, but generally tend to remain tolerant despite the irritation.

FEELS DEEPLY, FINDS   versus   EMOTIONAL
EXPRESSION OF FEELINGS   AND EXPRESSIVE
DIFFICULT

Yellow teenage girl: (frustrated and pleading) "But why won't you come
                         and have dinner with my parents? They want so much
                         to meet you!"

White teenage boy: (frustrated and quiet) "I really don't feel comfortable
                         meeting them yet. Maybe next month."

This White young man confided in me that he was afraid that his girlfriend's parents would ask him about his grades. He felt frustrated because they would be disappointed in him and resist their daughter's decision to date him in the future. Rather than be honest with her or them, he chose to simply avoid communication all together and stay away.

Whites often think deeply but choose not to say most things because they feel awkward in their verbal communication. Instead, they ponder their feelings inside and share very little. Yellows get upset and emotional and say what they feel regardless of how eloquent it may or may not be. Yellows need to express themselves and hear what their White friends feel as well.

Yellows must learn to be patient with Whites. Whites appreciate Yellows just sitting with them without expectation that Whites should speak. Whites require time to observe others. When they feel accepted, they are more likely to express themselves.

DOER   versus   DELEGATOR/PERFORMER

Whites are Indians rather than Indian Chiefs. They are not interested in great fanfare and complication. They generally feel more comfortable doing the work rather than delegating it to others. Whites are not strong verbal communicators which typically limits their managerial skills. However, when Whites feel comfortable with these skills, they make excellent delegators due to their patience, tact and tolerance for other employees.

Yellows like center stage. They enjoy opportunities to perform (please, no routine housework) and willingly delegate mundane work and details to others. Yellows are charismatic leaders with poor follow-through. They are dynamic motivators and often find themselves in the spot-light regardless of their actual job title. Whites and Yellows usually work well together because their role preferences lie in different directions.

PATIENT   versus   GOOD NATURED

Two best friends spent a lot of their time together throughout their college careers. They were roommates and would often get together on campus to eat together, see a movie or study at the library. The White roommate would typically arrive up to one hour later than agreed upon. His Yellow friend would usually find a quiet place and study or run into a friend and share some good laughs while he waited. They never became angry with each other. They simply ate later or took in a later movie. If the Yellow became bored he would simply go ahead alone, and neither was upset or concerned.

Yellows and Whites enjoy a rare capacity for tolerance and acceptance no other mixed color combination share. Both are slow to anger and quick to move on when slighted.

NON-POSSESSIVE   versus   NON-POSSESSIVE
(unless threatened)

Neither personality is usually driven by a need to possess people or material things. Yellows live for the moment, rarely save money, and simply need enough money to survive. Yellows can always make new friends and, subsequently, rarely feel threatened by losing people in their life. They can't really imagine losing friends, spouses or children because so many people are so easily drawn to them throughout life.

Whites are gentle in their approach to other people. Whites are sometimes overwhelmed if they feel rejected by another person and don't know how to respond. Whites typically have little concern for monetary advantages. They are easily satisfied and usually unwilling to expend the necessary energy required to "beat the competition" and climb the ladder of "corporate success."

White-Yellow combinations are very relaxed with each other. Neither places much demand on the other person. Both are willing to live on less because their relationship is often comfortable without the pressure of always having to *be* or *have* more.

COMPLIANT WITH RULES   versus   DEFIANT TO RULES

Whites tend to obey laws, rules, regulations and authority figures. Yellows often disobey laws, rules, regulations and authority figures. This disparity can create tension between White and Yellows. However, Whites are so tolerant and tactful that they can often convince Yellows to rethink their unacceptable behavior. Yellows are sensitive to social approval. Despite their zest for doing "wild and crazy" things, they are receptive to positive social influences by those they value and respect.

FORGIVING BUT   versus   FORGIVING
REMEMBERS

Both personalities are very forgiving. They tend to accept that everyone makes mistakes. Neither typically wastes much energy on "yesterday's news." Whites, however, are more likely to remember when they were crossed and steer clear of any similar situation that appears to be potentially endangering. Whites are also known to feel deeply transgressions against them but generally find their motive of peace so dominant that it overrides the attitude of retribution.

Yellows forgive quickly and without great time delays. One Yellow woman shared a very personal problem with a White friend who, in turn, shared it with others. The Yellow was terribly hurt but acknowledged not more than one day later she would most likely share personal information with the same friend again.

Whites and Yellows rarely burden their relationship with emotional garbage. They focus on the positive aspects of each other's personality and appreciate each one's unique contribution.

OVERWHELMED   versus   POSITIVE

When crises arise Whites often feel overwhelmed. Yellows typically see the silver lining in the dark clouds. Whites are vulnerable to seeing only a few options when seeking solutions. Yellows often find unlimited possibilities. Whites *seek* magical rescuers (i.e., "the White knight syndrome") while Yellows *feel* magical in problem resolution. Typically Whites reflect the pessimist and Yellows assume the role of the optimist.

DEDICATED ONLY   versus   LACKS DISCIPLINE
WHEN INTERESTED

Whites are particular about their commitments. They can be lazy and do not necessarily feel any compulsion to constantly be productive. With this relaxed attitude, Whites find it difficult to commit themselves to people or activities which have little or no interest for them. Whites are often difficult to motivate and keep motivated in various relationships and hobbies. Yellow parents and spouses are often frustrated in getting White children and companions to take responsibility for themselves or stay interested in something. However, once a White connects with some activity or work assignment, they are generally dedicated and loyal.

Yellows stumble throughout life over the word discipline. Consistency is a word rather foreign to Yellows. They tend to stay with something as long as it is fun. Most achievements in life require a commitment of consistent effort and pain. Fun is not typically a major ingredient in the initial stages of achievement. This explains why many Yellows settle for the simple life. They prefer to play and often lack the appreciation and commitment of stretching.

EXCELLENT LISTENER   versus   POOR LISTENER

Yellows are restless and Whites are calm. Listening requires patience and the willingness to put others before oneself. Yellows tend to do neither well. Whites are comfortable sitting with another person for hours while they share every detail of how they feel. Yellows constantly interrupt and sense no reverence for the art of listening. Yellows hurry the conversation along, often finishing the speaker's sentence. Whites enjoy a slower pace and encourage the speaker to move at his pace accepting long pauses without questioning or rushing the thoughts. Whites find Yellows quite abrasive in this behavior and tend to stay quiet until (or unless) the Yellow learns to appreciate and practice the art of listening.

BLAMES SELF   versus   BLAMES OTHERS

When something negative happens, Whites usually blame themselves and Yellows blame others. The following conversation reflects their styles.

White: "How could I have been so stupid? I should have handled it differently."

Yellow: "Why didn't you take care of the problem. You should have handled it differently!"

Neither response is positive. Whites often struggle with low self-esteem because they assume responsibility for creating (or at least contributing to) most problems. Yellows are naively over-confident and tend to be limited in their emotional growth because they assume no responsibility for creating or contributing to most problems.

TOO SENSITIVE   versus   INSENSITIVE

Whites tend to feel bad easily. They are especially vulnerable to Yellow's flippant remarks and overall naive insensitivity. Yellows do not think of other's feelings when they make rude or playful comments. Whites are not inclined to verbally respond. They are more likely to hold the pain inside and quietly shy away from further social interaction. Often Whites silently blame themselves and simultaneously feel hurt that others don't understand their frustration. Yellows typically misread White's behavior as "They're okay. They're always quiet like that." Yellows do not pay much attention to other's needs or behaviors as long as Yellows are having a good time. They are often totally surprised to find out later that they have offended Whites at all.

MAKING THE MOST OF COMFORTABLE OPPOSITES

WHITES NEED YELLOWS:	YELLOWS NEED WHITES:
To excite them	To calm them
To encourage them	To listen to them
To accept their low profile	To praise them
To be kind to them	To play with them
To slow down	To speed up
To be intimate with them	To be tolerant of them
To keep confidences	To share confidences
To promote activities	To enjoy their childlike innocence
To share a peaceful relationship	To share a peaceful relationship
To be sensitive of their self-doubts	To accept their crazy spontaneity

POTENTIAL CONFLICTS OF COMFORTABLE OPPOSITES

WHITES	YELLOWS
Non-verbal	Craves praise
Directionless	Directionless
Passive	Passionate
Enjoys private time	Likes social scene
Lackadaisical	Lackadaisical
Soft spoken	Verbal and loud
Quietly appropriate	Obnoxious
Boring	Exciting

Sparkle and Shine

YELLOW-YELLOW RELATIONSHIPS

Yellow-Yellow relationships are as obvious as neon lights on a poorly lighted street corner at night. They sparkle and shine for everyone to see. People rarely mistake this combination for anyone else. Like two playful pups, they chase each other through life oblivious to the rest of the world around them. They are playful and fun. This combination definitely knows how to have a good time.

Yellows enjoy their mutual friendships. They are not typically drawn to each other in committed marital relationships because of the word "committed." Friendships are generally convenient while marriage is not. As long as two Yellows can get themselves to the same place at the same time, they will always enjoy a "good time" together. Marriage requires much more than merely agreeing on a place and time. Someone has to tell the playful pups when the work needs to get done. When there *is no one else* but the playful pups, they rarely prioritize a healthy balance between work and play.

Yellows live on raw energy. They can typically go for hours without revitalizing themselves. They travel well together. They party well together. They laugh well together. What they don't do well together is work—homework, housework, or detailed deadline work. They are both easily distracted from labor and easily find numerous reasons for why it is an excellent time to take a break from the rigors of work. They focus their energy on playful productivity including recreation, conversation and creative exploration. They prefer to use their energy in twos or more, rarely opting to be alone.

Yellow-Yellow combinations draw people to them like magnets. They are leaders and yet, tend to be overwhelmed once they attract the interest of others. They lead most comfortably in play activity. Subsequently, their greatest influence on others is most often expressed in the playful world of fun.

FUN

Yellow-Yellow combinations generally agree that "the more people there are, the merrier time they'll enjoy." They want to share their fun with everyone as long as others don't become too demanding of their time. They also struggle with people who are too conventional in their thinking. Yellow-Yellows rarely place limits on their fun zone in their relationship. As long as everyone is having a good time, everything else can wait. *This relationship shares the fantasy that all roads eventually lead to Disneyland, a ski resort or the beach.*

NEEDS ATTENTION

Both require a lot of each other's attention. Actually, this is quite easily accomplished because Yellows seek instant and simple praise rather than deep appreciation. They are naturally optimistic and giving each other generally positive praise is easily accomplished. They can accommodate each other's needs by pausing briefly in their "self-centered" monologues to notice each other before continuing on with their self-presentations. Neither is generally offended or concerned with this limited attention. Having a good time and upbeat praise is usually enough to keep Yellow-Yellows from feeling neglected in the relationship.

FREEDOM

This combination regards freedom as a sacred principle in their relationship. Neither tries to attach strings or commitment (a less than sacred word) to each other. Yellow friends accept whatever time they have to share together and share it to the fullest. Neither wants or intends to commit to much beyond the present. Yellows can drop out of each other's lives for years and easily pick up where they left off when they get together again. They don't feel neglected or particularly frustrated by the lack of effort to keep in touch through the years. Both value their freedom to move in and out of the relationship and don't attach strings to their commitments. They are more likely to simply accept each other at face value.

HIGHLY VERBAL

Talk, talk, talk!!! Yellows can talk about everything or nothing equally well. They appreciate superficial and serious discussions. Put them in a party, at a funeral or in their kitchen and they will find things to converse about. Neither is strong on listening skills which doesn't seem to deter their interest in conversation. However, it does preclude much depth or meaningful direction in ongoing relationships since they often miss many important insights due to poor listening skills. Constant dialogue is not lacking in their relationship and both willingly share responsibility for promoting and sustaining positive chatter.

UNCOMMITTED

This color combinations promotes play and fears commitment. They have the perception that freedom and playful activity are necessarily incompatible with commitment. In light of this dilemma, Yellow relationships typically choose their freedom and neglect commitments. This attitude makes interaction of an intimate or responsible nature improbable. They typically "wear out" before the end, which is disappointing in relationships requiring a long, enduring commitment.

IRRESPONSIBLE

Yellows typically expect others to "handle the details and cover the loose ends." When the other person is another Yellow, "the details are often neglected and loose ends never tied together." Neither takes their roles very seriously and, subsequently, their relationship often struggles with last minute mix-ups, and other irresponsible problems which reduce the quality of their shared life experience.

This is well illustrated by two Yellow friends who were babysitting together one evening. The girl fell asleep at 5:00 p.m. and woke up at 7:00 p.m. Meanwhile, her friend had popped popcorn. He and the kids were enjoying popcorn and a movie when she awoke. She assumed they had already eaten dinner since they were eating popcorn. He assumed popcorn was enough. Needless to say, neither was asked to babysit again. Ignoring details is not always serious but repeated negligence can be terribly inappropriate, if not life threatening.

OPTIMISTIC

This color combination believes most anything can be accomplished with time or help or something—perhaps, just hope. They are eternal dreamers and optimists. They always seek the silver lining in the cloud or find some value in the pit inside a cherry. Pollyanna times two is a tough challenge for anyone to face. Yellows don't get depressed easily and if they do, they don't stay depressed for long. In a Yellow-Yellow relationship, both support and build each other with hope and positive reinforcement.

CURIOUS AND INQUISITIVE

Yellows ask the darndest questions at the darndest times. They simply want to know things and usually forget important social protocol when asking. The answers are not typically as important as the process of discovering the answers. Yellows find it great fun in looking for clues to explain human behavior. They typically enjoy each other's free spirited (often bordering on the obnoxious) pursuit of insight and understanding.

ENTERTAINING

Yellows love to entertain each other and be entertained by each other. They are performers. They entice each other with spontaneous surprises (i.e., show tickets, weekend retreats, cards or flowers). They enjoy carefree experiences and light moments of laughter and intimacy. This combination is far more inclined to spend money and time on action-filled opportunities (i.e., trips and recreation) than material possessions (i.e., expensive gifts and household fixtures). They live for the present and both appreciate entertaining experiences that facilitate immediate pleasures.

Yellow-Yellow combinations adore each other. They value their relationship and find each other spontaneous and refreshing. They enjoy their freedom and struggle with necessary commitments and responsible behavior. This combination lives for today with little interest in yesterday's regrets or tomorrow's concerns. Yellows gravitate toward each other and often remain playful companions for life. They casually enter and exit each other's lives with little concern for long-term impact.

This combination loves life best when it is shared with others. They appreciate each other's positive and hopeful natures. They are fun and superficially attentive to each other. Intimacy remains an important, yet fleeting, concern in a Yellow-Yellow relationship. They value their connection to other people and particularly enjoy sharing special moments with other Yellows, like themselves.

Spunky and highly verbal, Yellows vitalize each other with constant chatter and inquisitive interaction. These shared behavior styles make this combination an enjoyable treat to observe. In the long run, Yellow-Yellow connections are enviable playmates but unlikely marital companions. Whatever relationship they experience together will never be dull or lack excitement. They are a fun, dynamic duo who vigorously pursue "the good life" with refreshing curiosity and optimism.

Life is a series of mountains to climb. *The Color Code* is simply a beginning. It may, however, represent a significant step in your life's journey. The sudden identity you have experienced as a Red, Blue, White or Yellow may encourage further questions and insights about your life. You have identified how your color fits in the puzzle of relationships. You may want further help in addressing concerns you struggle with in the process of mixing colors and creating your rainbow connections.

During every mountain climbing experience, wild flowers and beautiful sunsets exist. They are available for every climber to see and enjoy. They represent truths in all of our lives. Whether we choose to see them or not, they exist. Truths in life, like wild flowers and sunsets on our mountain climb can be pointed out—taught. If we refuse to see them, however, we must remain ignorant and blind. Yes, we will still climb the mountain, but the quality of our mountain climbing experience remains limited and disappointing.

As we go through life, superficial people may ask us to lead them up the mountain, knowing we have been there before. Limited by our own choosing, we can only take them directly to the top, unable to see and point out the wild flowers and beautiful sunsets we have neglected to see ourselves on previous climbs. Until we choose to see and hear quality truths in life, we necessarily remain unable to offer them to others.

Quality people (whether they come in the role of parent, child, friend, lover, or employer) demand a more balanced mountain climbing experience. Yes, they desire to reach the top. And yet, for them the climb must include the truths and available beautiful aspects they instinctively "know" or have been taught can be experienced on the climb, as well. Merely surviving the ordeal will never suffice. They expect to fully live their lives, herein symbolized by a mountain climb.

Our personal happiness and success at building our character will be determined by our willingness to observe, conceptualize and apply what we learn. Depth, breadth and height are gained accordingly. Limitations are primarily placed on us by ourselves. If our goals are flexible and our expectations are reasonable we can attain and maintain a positive self-image.

Look to your journey as the ultimate purpose of life. We can never relive our lives quite the same as we do today. As we look within ourselves and identify who we are, we can feel joy in knowing we have substance and value. We can commit to replacing personality limitations with charactered life principles. We can commit to relationships with passion and feel the strength expressed in the rainbow connection. The first step is being able to say, "I know who I am and what I am, and I know who and what I want to become." These perceptions may change with our growth process, but the essential attitudes of humility and positive goal setting remain as healthy catalysts in our life journey.

A common sign of an unhealthy person is defensiveness. Insecure people are barely treading water in life. Consequently, having to deal with a new color (one with explicit limitations as well as strengths) often overwhelms a weaker person and causes them to resist any new and challenging input. I find these people to be *frightened individuals* who "refuse to be labeled" or see themselves as "flawed" in any way. They may react to new information about themselves with any number of attitudes and/or behaviors. Common defenses include: attacking the presenter of the material, ignoring the material, quickly pointing out a "friend" who could really use the information, pretending to accept the material but with no intentions of pursuing it in their lives, or suggesting the timing is somewhat difficult and they will get back to you when there is a better time to discuss it.

Unfortunately, they are reacting the only way they know. They are simply protecting the little self-regard they feel is left in them. If only they would risk that "little self-regard" in order to see the vast self-love they could generate if they would just invest the effort. We all deserve to travel through life with an abundance of self-love, rich with positive experiences and caring friends and family. Defensive people only limit themselves from what they deserve. They will discover that only when they are willing to see themselves accurately and get on with the process of growing up (character building), can they experience the mountain climb at its best.

While reading *The Color Code,* you have experienced a sudden identity and your journey to self-actualization has begun. With your commitment to developing your new identity you will experience many opportunities to appreciate yourself and others. Life's greatest moments are never more clearly experienced than in our genuine connection to ourselves and others. Our success come with these rare, yet magical moments. These moments occur repeatedly throughout our lives as we honestly assess ourselves and lovingly value others.

Unconditional love is experienced when we accept and promote others as *they* wish to be accepted and promoted. Loving requires trusting and risking. Loving allows for the limitations of those we love. It prevents our expectations from exceeding the abilities of the ones we love. We must believe in other's ability to make healthy decisions. We accept and promote their choices, regardless, at times, of how healthy or unhealthy their choices may be.

While there are occasions when criticism is appropriate and helpful, it must always stem from a clean motive in order to impact the individual for whom the criticism is intended. We must care and truly value the individual before we are in a position to offer a critique.

Enjoy your climb up the mountain. I have enjoyed the part of the trip that we have made together. As a Yellow, it has been challenging to commit myself so completely to a task other than play. As with anything worthwhile, the prices are high, but the sunsets—yes, the sunsets have been even more rewarding than I could have dreamed.

I value intimacy, learning and creating new insights. Unfortunately, distributing my thoughts in a book is less personal than I prefer. However, I would invite your feedback so that I can share in your life's journey as you have shared in mine. Happy mountain climbing. I hope that we will continue to cross each other's paths along our ascent to the top.

It takes a lot of colors to make a rainbow. It takes a lot of people to make a book.

My life is a rainbow filled with very special family, friends and teachers, who have continually colored my world with truths, passions and love.

My book is a mutual tribute to the many individuals who have contributed so freely of their talents. My four Red friends helped take this whole project from the dream phase to reality. Linda Burhansstipanov, Charles Hansen, Tish Whitney and Pierre Droubay inspired me and demanded that I perspire, as well. (So it goes with Reds, right!) They always believed in me and the book. Spider (Mary) Portis (White), and Terri Krasho (Blue), brought peaceful repose in an otherwise, harried and confusing process. My wife, Jean (Blue), and our children, (Terra and BreAnne (Reds), Summer (Blue), and Mikelle (Yellow) never let me lose the proper perspective of positive, colorful relationships. Finally, my patients (all colors) freely assisted in my research, by inviting me to share in their lives and rewarding me with their love. I love and appreciate you all.

For Additional Copies, please write

Taylor Hartman, Ph.D.
P.O. Box 87
Trabuco Canyon, California 92678

RECOMMENDED RESOURCE MATERIALS AVAILABLE
FROM COLOR CODE COMMUNCATIONS, INC.

<u>The Color Code</u> by Taylor Hartman, Ph.D. Hardback copies are $19.95 (Utah residents add $1.25 tax). Softback copies are $14.95 (Utah residents add $.93 tax). The most accurate literature available on personalities and relationships. Inspires and motivates quality lifestyling. Vital to understanding personal development and successful interpersonal relationships.

<u>The Character Code</u> by Taylor Hartman, Ph.D. $19.95 (Utah residents add $1.25 tax). (Hardback only). The most revolutionary psycho-social-spiritual book available on becoming a fully charactered individual. Presented with refreshing candor and professionalism, this six step guide provides tremendous counsel for identifying and embracing a quality life.

<u>Hartman Personality Profile</u> $1.00 (includes tax) Professionally designed profile includes explanation for self-administration and self-scoring for results. An overview of the basic personality types is provided for each participant's review.

<u>Hartman Character Profile</u> $1.00 (includes tax) Professionally designed profile provides opportunity to determine each individual's current status of character.

Includes explanation for self-administration and results of the Profile.

<u>Dealing Effectively With Different Personalities</u> $49.95 (Utah residents add $3.12 tax). Powerful six-hour cassette program complete with excellent recommendations for understanding and successfully relating to each individual color. Numerous examples are provided to assist you in immediate appreciation. Four tapes focus on each of the four color personalities. The Color Code Cassette includes unparalleled live presentation of sheer enjoyment. Humorous in delivery and bold in content, it offers a candid overview of his life-impacting theory. The Character Code Cassette presents years of clinical experience with sincere enthusiasm in reviewing Dr. Hartman's powerful six step program on becoming a charactered individual. For this often dysfunctional world of business and personal relationships, this tape is a must for anyone seeking to apply the Concepts of The Color Code.

<u>The Knight in Rusty Armor</u> by David Fisher $5.00 (Utah residents add $.31 tax). Delightful story about a knight who saves the world and loses his family. This book takes a light-hearted path in presenting rich insights about priorities, relationships, and truth.

Telephone Orders: Visa/MC (801) 565-9559. We have secretarial staff and 24-hour voice mail to assist you in ordering materials. Please leave your name, mailing address, daytime telephone number, Visa or MC number, expiration date and specify requested materials. Merchandise is mailed within three working days.

Mail Orders: Send order form, checks or Visa/MC number to: Color Code Communications, Inc., 3853 East Little Cottonwood Lane, Sandy, Utah 84092
**Make checks payable to Color Code Communications, Inc.

Color Code Communications, Inc. stands behind all of our products. If, for any reason, you are not satisfied with any product, simply return the merchandise in 30 days and you will receive a full refund. We are in the people building business because we believe in ourselves and the people we serve.

Quantity	Description	Price	Amount

Name		Shp/hand	$ 3.00
Address		**Sub Total**	$
City, State, Zip		Sales Tax	$
Telephone ( )		**TOTAL**	$

COLOR CODE COMMUNICATIONS, INC.
PROGRAMS AND SERVICES

PUBLIC/INHOUSE SEMINARS

Color Code Communications, Inc., specializes in offering half-day, one and two-day seminars as well as customized business inhouse training programs. These seminars concentrate on developing people through focused communications, genuine character, and passionate purpose. Powerfully motivating, this training offers immediate application for every participant.

COMMUNITY/BUSINESS LECTURES

In high demand as speakers, Dr. Hartman and his trained consultants offer speeches for different occasions on a variety of topics. These one to two hour presentations offer engaging entertainment balanced with much food for thought.

PERSONAL/PROFESSIONAL RETREATS

These three-day experiences held in the majestic mountains of Sundance, Utah, generate renewed personal vision and professional commitment. Limited to only ten participants, this unique retreat opportunity is offered to individuals for personal reflection and insights as well as professional colleagues for team building and professional interaction. Based on Color Code Theory, this retreat experience delves into personal strengths and limitations, establishing positive affirmations, developing clean motives, and learning to deal effectively with other people. Personal retreat experiences are offered to individuals, while the professional retreat experience is offered as a package to interested businesses.

INDIVIDUAL CONSULTANT TRAINING

Color Code Communications, Inc. offers training for independent training consultants twice a year. This intensive three-day program provides information on content only which can then be adapted to specialized needs. Interested individuals must be dynamic presenters with experience in the training field.

CORPORATE TRAIN-THE-TRAINER PROGRAM

Many corporations seek permission to utilize Color Code Communication's resource materials and training. We provide an opportunity for inhouse representatives to be trained to present the Color Code Communications concepts and philosophy within their organization. Our training is presented in a way that will enable them to adapt it to their particular needs whether it be communication, leadership and management, stress reduction, supervision, hiring, firing and other personnel concerns, etc.

FOR ADDITIONAL INFORMATION ON ANY OF THESE PROGRAMS OR SERVICES, PLEASE CALL (801) 942-5803 OR WRITE TO COLOR CODE COMMUNICATIONS, INC., ATTENTION MARKETING DEPARTMENT, AT 3853 EAST LITTLE COTTONWOOD LANE, SANDY, UTAH 84092.